Quick Reference
Guide

Windows® 98

Karl Schwartz
Candi Dickerson

DDC *Publishing*

275 Madison Avenue
New York, NY 10016

Published by DDC Publishing, Inc.

DDC Publishing
275 Madison Avenue
New York, New York 10016
Phone: 800-528-3897
Fax: 800-528-3862
http://www.ddcpub.com

First DDC Publishing Printing
10   9   8   7   6   5   4   3   2   1

Catalog No. G35

ISBN: 1-56243-583-3

Printed in the United States of America

ACKNOWLEDGEMENTS

Thank you Joanne, for your support and awesome courage.

KS

Thank you, Cathy, for the crash course in style issues.
Thank you, Kathy and Julie, for the patience and encouragement.
Thank you, Nikki and Michael, for sticking with me.

CJD

Authors:	Karl Schwartz
	Candi Dickerson
Managing Editor:	Kathy Berkemeyer
English Editors:	Nicole Bowman
	Rebecca J. Fiala
	Cathy Vesecky
Technical Editor:	Michael Dickerson
Layout:	Julie Janssen

INTRODUCTION

CONVENTIONS

Command Examples

Procedures in this guide are generally composed of a series of numbered steps. To complete a procedure, it is necessary to complete the steps in sequential order. As shown in the example below, you usually have a choice of both mouse and keyboard methods to complete a step. In many instances, these methods are combined, as in the following example:

1 Click <u>F</u>ile menu .... `Alt` + `F`

*This step indicates that you can access the **File** menu either by clicking on its name in the menu bar, or by holding down the **Alt** key while pressing the F key.*

*In cases where multiple mouse and keystroke methods are shown for one task, the commands are either broken down into separate subheadings (e.g., **Use Address Bar to Access a Site** or **Use Go Menu to Access a Site**), or they are divided by the word **OR**, as below:*

Click **Copy** toolbar button ....

OR

a Click <u>E</u>dit menu .... `Alt` + `E`

b Click <u>C</u>opy .... `C`

As shown in the example above, mouse steps generally appear first followed by the corresponding keystrokes.

*Keystrokes are listed to the right of steps in reverse type (e.g., `Alt`+`F`). Although this manual shows these keyboard characters in uppercase letters, they should be typed in lowercase; there is no need to press the **Shift** key unless specifically instructed to do so. When you see a substitution word to the right of a step, (e.g., text), replace it with the required value, such as a filename password.*

INTRODUCTION

The Web browsing style, not the Classic browsing style, is used throughout this Quick Reference Guide. The Web browsing style changes the mouse clicking procedures: point to (not click) an item to select it; click (not double-click) an item to activate it.

When selecting commands in Windows 98 common dialog boxes, you can often activate them by double-clicking. Also, number settings can often be increased or decreased by clicking scroll arrows. Note that these procedures are not always illustrated in this manual.

The Windows key *is new to this Quick Reference Guide. This modifier key is found on the Windows 95-ready keyboard.*

In addition to the command procedures included in this Quick Reference Guide, other techniques for executing a given task often exist. The techniques listed here represent the easiest, most commonly used procedures.

The following graphics will alert you to important hints:

    💣   *Caution*

    📖   *Note*

    ✓   *Tip*

ACTION WORDS

Five verbs are consistently used throughout this guide to indicate specific actions. You can:

- ***Click** a menu item or button.*
- ***Point to** an item without clicking the mouse.*
- ***Select** an item from a drop-down list, a check box item, or an option button in a dialog box.*
- ***Press** a keyboard key.*
- ***Type** information.*

Introduction

WINDOWS 3.1 UPGRADE TIPS

Start Programs

Use the Start menu on the taskbar.

Program items that were stored in groups will be found
in the **Programs** folder in the **Start** menu.

- Click **Start**, point to **Programs**, point to the desired folder
  name (the Windows 3.1 group name), then click the
  desired application.

  See The Start Menu, page 8.
  See Open Applications Using Start Menu, page 53.

Start MS-DOS Programs

Use the Start menu on the taskbar.

You can open the MS-DOS Prompt from the **Programs**
folder in the **Start** menu.

- Click **Start**, point to **Programs**, then click **MS-DOS
  Prompt**.

  See MS-DOS Applications, page 61.

Manage Files

*Perform file operations with Windows Explorer or from any
folder window.*

The **My Computer** folder contains all the drives on your computer.
Windows Explorer is similar to File Manager; however, it displays the
entire hierarchy of all folders in the left pane (including system folders
and network drives). You can perform folder and file operations from
any folder window that you open through the **My Computer** folder
or from Windows Explorer.

- **To open My Computer:** Click the **My Computer** icon on
  the desktop, then click the drive you wish to browse.

- **To open Windows Explorer:** Click **Start**, point to
  Programs, then click **Windows Explorer**.

See Control Panel Settings

Open Control Panel from the Start menu on the taskbar.

The **Control Panel** contains tools that let you set system settings, such as Display, Printers, and Sound.

- Click the **Start** button, point to **Settings**, then click **Control Panel**.

  *See **Control Panel**, page 15.*

Switch Between Running Applications

Switch to the desired application or folder button on the taskbar.

Each application or folder you open appears as a button on the taskbar.

- Click the application or folder button on the taskbar.

  *See **Switch Tasks**, page 60.*

Change Web Style Browsing Style

By default, Web style browsing is in effect.

With Web style browsing enabled you need only to point to an item to select it, or click an item to open it. Windows 98 lets you easily change the browsing style to the Classic (double-click) style, or you can customize browsing as desired.

- Click the **Start** button, point to **Settings**, then click **Folder Options**.

INTRODUCTION

WINDOWS 95 UPGRADE TIPS

Use the Active Desktop

Bring the Web to your desktop.

The Active Desktop adds a Web layer to the standard desktop so you can display Web items such as headlines for breaking news stories, tickers for stock quotes, and weather reports.

- Click **Start**, point to **Settings**, point to **Active Desktop,** then click **View as Web Page**.

Add Toolbars to the Taskbar

Customize the taskbar.

Add toolbars to your Windows taskbar, making it even easier to get to your programs, files, folders, subscriptions, and favorite Web pages.

- Right-click the taskbar, point to **Toolbars**, then click the toolbar you want to add.

Browse Your Computer Like the Web

By default, Web style browsing is in effect.

*With Web style browsing enabled, you can click the **Back** and **Forward** buttons on the Standard toolbar to view folders you have previously opened. Use the **Up** button to view the next folder up in the hierarchy of folders.*

- Click the **Start** button, point to **Settings**, click **Folder**

Options, then select **Web style**.

See *Browse Using Folder Windows*, page 139.
See *Change Folder Browsing Style*, page 133.
See *Standard Folder Toolbar*, page 130.
See *Customize Folder Appearance*, page 133.
See *View Previously Opened Folders or Web Sites*, page 141.

Use the Favorites Folder from Folder Windows

Open your favorite sites from anywhere on your computer.

The **Favorites** folder is available from the **Start** menu and from folder window menu bars.

- **From the desktop:** Click **Start**, point to **Favorites**, then click the desired link.
- **From a folder window:** Click the **Favorites** menu, then click a favorite site.
  See *Favorites Folder*, page 193.

Use the Go Menu

Go to selected sites from this new folder window menu.

From the **Go** menu, you can access your Internet home page, check your e-mail, search the Web, or go directly to the **My Computer** folder.

- Click the **Go** menu in a folder window, then click the desired site from the list.
  See *Use Go Menu to Access a Site*, page 182.

Web Style Browsing Style

By default, Web style browsing is in effect.

With Web style browsing enabled, you need only to point to an item to select it, or click an item to open it. Windows 98 lets you easily change the browsing style to the Classic (double-click) style, or you can customize browsing as desired.

- Click the **Start** button, point to **Settings**, then click **Folder Options**.

INTRODUCTION

*See **Basic Mouse Skills**, page 4.*
*See **Browse Using Folder Windows**, page 139.*
*See **Browse Using Windows Explorer**, page 140.*
*See **Select Folders and Files**, page 166.*
*See **Change Folder Browsing Style**, page 133.*

SETUP NOTES

The new Windows setup is smoother and easier than ever before. However, if you carry out the recommendations that follow, you will reduce the risk of setup failures, and you'll be prepared to recover data if problems do occur.

Before Installing Windows 98

First print and read the Setup text file on the Windows 98 CD.

✓ Print the file and read the information that pertains to your system.

More information on the following recommendations can be found in the Setup text file.

✓ Be sure you have enough free disk space (between 120 MB to 355 MB).

✓ Disable all antivirus programs.

✓ Disable unnecessary TSRs (Terminate and Stay Ready programs) that are typically loaded by AUTOEXEC.BAT.

✓ Prepare an MS-DOS boot disk that lets you access your CD-ROM drive.

✓ Run ScanDisk (in Thorough mode) to check and fix disk errors.

✓ Close all running applications.

When Installing Windows 98

✓ Create a new startup disk when prompted.

This disk can help you continue the Setup process if it is interrupted.

TABLE OF CONTENTS

TABLE OF CONTENTS

GETTING STARTED

START AND QUIT WINDOWS

When you start Windows, you may see a prompt to log on to Windows and/or a network. When you shut down, Windows saves settings, such as the positions of icons on your desktop.

Start Windows

📖 *To access the Windows 98 startup menu, restart or start your computer, then press and hold* **Ctrl** *(or press* **F8** *for some machines) when your computer begins to boot (access the hard disk).*

1 Turn on your computer system.

Windows will start automatically. Depending on the speed of your system, it may take a few minutes or more for Windows to load into your computer's memory.

📖 *If a* **Welcome to Windows** *prompt appears, type a user name and password. Windows will provide a second prompt to confirm your password. If you leave the password blank, Windows will not prompt you to log on the next time Windows starts.*

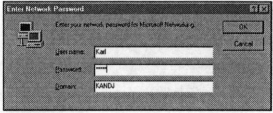

2 Type your name...*name*
in **User name** text box, if necessary.

3 Type a password.........................**Alt** + **P**, *password*
in **Password** text box.

continued...

Getting Started

Start Windows (cont.)

4 Type a valid domain name .... **Alt** + **D**, *domain name*
   or the name of your login server in
   Domain text box, if necessary.

> 📖 *Consult your network administrator for the domain
> name or server name, if required.*

5 Click OK ....**Enter**

Restart Your Computer

*You may want to restart your computer when you have encountered
error messages, if programs perform erratically, or if your system
begins to slow down. Before restarting, Windows may prompt you to
save data if Windows applications are open. However, Windows
cannot close MS-DOS applications automatically. You should switch
to those programs (see **Switch Tasks**, page 60) and exit them before
restarting or shutting down Windows.*

1 Click **Start** on taskbar .... **Ctrl** + **Esc**

   OR

   Press **Alt** while pressing **S** .... **Alt** + **S**

   OR

   Press the **Windows** key .... 🪟

2 Click **Shut Down** .... 📄 Shut Down...

3 Click **Restart** option button.. **R**

4 Click OK ....**Enter**

> 📖 *Use the following procedure if system instability
> prevents you from restarting your computer, or exiting
> an MS-DOS application.*

GETTING STARTED

Restart Using Ctrl+Alt+Del

*This will display the **Close Program** dialog box from which you can
close a program by selecting it and clicking* EndTask *, or you can
shut down Windows by clicking* Shut Down...

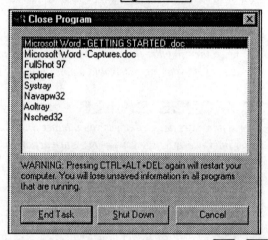

- Press **Ctrl+Alt+Del** .... Ctrl + Alt + Delete

Shut Down Your Computer

1 Click Start ....

2 Click **Sh_ut Down** .... Shut Down...

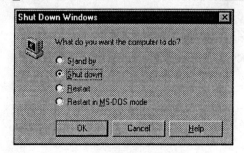

continued...

GETTING STARTED

Shut Down Your Computer (cont.)

3 Click **Shut down** option button...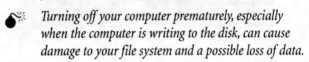

4 Click [OK   ]..Enter

5 Wait for Windows to display a message that it is safe to turn off your computer, then turn off your computer and monitor.

> 💣 *Turning off your computer prematurely, especially when the computer is writing to the disk, can cause damage to your file system and a possible loss of data.*

BASIC MOUSE SKILLS

*The **mouse** is a hardware device that lets you interact with Windows' graphical user interface by letting you perform such actions as pointing, clicking, and dragging.*

> 📖 *Clicking is usually done with the left mouse button. You can change the following mouse settings from the Control Panel (see **Set Mouse Properties**, page 122): primary mouse button (for left-handed users), double-click speed, pointer speed, and show pointer trails.*

Point to an Item

- Move mouse until pointer is on item.

Click an Item

1 Point to item.

2 Press and release *left* **mouse button** once to select or activate item.

GETTING STARTED

Double-Click an Item

1 Point to item.

2 Press and release *left* **mouse button** twice in rapid
   succession to select or activate item.

Drag an Item

*This action is sometimes called **drag and drop**.*

1 Point to item.

2 Press and hold *left* **mouse button** while moving mouse.

   As you move the mouse, the item will move.

3 Release **mouse button** to drop item
   and complete the move.

Right-Click an Item

1 Point to item.

2 Press and release *right* **mouse button**.

3 Select desired option from shortcut menu that appears.

Getting Started

Right-Drag an Item

1 Point to item.

2 Press and hold *right* **mouse button** while moving mouse.

As you move the mouse, the item will move.

3 Release **mouse button** to drop item
and complete the move.

Default Mouse Pointer Scheme

*When you move the pointer, it will sometimes change to
indicate the kind of job it is doing. The following table shows the
default mouse pointer scheme for Windows 98.*

Shape	Name
	arrow (standard shape)
	sizing (sizes windows)
	move (moves windows)
	busy (signals for you to wait)
	hand (jumps between links)
	I-beam (text select)
	working in background (cursor is still active)
	Help select (shows tips about selected item)
	crosshair (precision select)
	unavailable (cannot perform action)

GETTING STARTED

Typical Mouse Actions

This table lists mouse actions for both the Web style and the Classic Windows environments. You can change the Windows environment so that a double-click will open an item. Procedures in this Quick Reference Guide will feature mouse actions for the Active Desktop. To select a browsing style, see **Change Folder Browsing Style**, *page 133.*

Objective:	Mouse Action:
Deselect item	Click empty area off item.
Close menu	Click anywhere off menu.
Copy file or folder	Press Ctrl and drag file/folder.
Go to link	Click underlined item.
Open menu	Click menu name.
Open shortcut menu	Right-click item.
Open submenu	Point to menu name.

A triangle ▶ next to a menu item means that a submenu follows.

Open item	*Web Style*: Click item.
	Classic Style: Double-click item.
Move file or folder	Press Shift and drag file/folder.
Position item	Drag item.
Select item	*Web Style*: Point to item.
	Classic Style: Click item.
Undo action	Right-click desktop, then click **Undo** on shortcut menu.

Open an Item's Properties Sheet

- Press **Alt** .... Alt +*double-click* and double-click desired item.

GETTING STARTED

Select Items

SELECT MULTIPLE ITEMS

1 Click or point to first item in group to select.

2 Press **Shift** and click or point to ....**Shift** +*last item*
last item in group to select.

SELECT SPECIFIC MULTIPLE ITEMS

- Press **Ctrl** and click or point to ....**Ctrl** +*select item*
individual items to select.

THE START MENU

*The **Start** button, when clicked, displays a menu that contains every-
thing you need to use Windows 98. By default, the **Start** button and
the taskbar are always visible. Therefore, you will always have access
to the commands and features you will need as you do your work.*

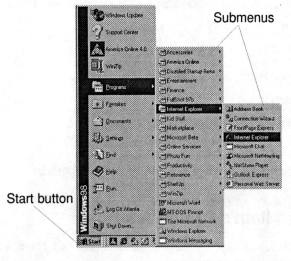

Submenus

Start button

WINDOWS 98
GETTING STARTED

Open Submenu on Start Menu

1 Click **Start** ....

2 Point to any menu item followed by a triangle ▶

Select Item on Start Menu

- Click desired item.

When you click an item that is not a submenu, a window or dialog box will open, and the name of the item will appear as a button on the taskbar.

> ✓ *Add an item to the Start menu by dragging its icon onto the Start button. See Add Items to Start Menu, page 103.*

Start Menu Items

Contains shortcuts to applications and application subfolders, such as the **Accessories** folder.

Contains shortcuts or links to Web sites you have added to the **Favorites** folder.

Contains shortcuts to recently used documents.

Provides access to the **Control Panel** folder, **Printers** folder, and **Taskbar & Start Menu Properties** dialog box. It also provides access to **Folder Options**, **Active Desktop**, and **Windows Update**.

Contains commands to find files, folders, computers, Internet sites, and people on the Internet.

Starts the online Help system for Windows 98.

continued...

GETTING STARTED

Start Menu Items (cont.)

 Opens a dialog box in which you can type a command to open programs, folders (including network folders), or Web sites.

 Lets you close all programs and log on as a different user.

 Provides shut down and restart options, including the option to restart in MS-DOS mode.

 *When you install Windows 98 software, a new folder for that software may appear in the **Programs** folder.*

GETTING STARTED

THE DESKTOP

*After starting Windows 98, you will see the **desktop**—the background area of your screen. The desktop is a root folder from which all items, in your computer and beyond, can be accessed.*

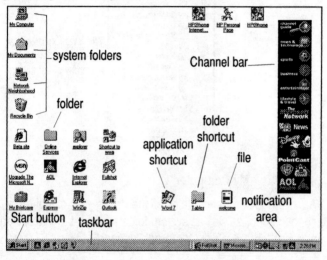

📖 *Windows 98 offers the option of an active desktop, pictured here. See **The Active Desktop**, page 74.*

*The desktop is a logical root folder that is physically on your hard disk. It is the top level of items in your computer system, including connections to other computers and the Internet. Because the desktop is a folder, you can store objects such as folders, shortcuts, and files there for fast access. The desktop has special properties that distinguish it from other folders. For example, you can set its properties to display a background color or an HTML (Web) document. See **Change Desktop Background**, page 82.*

GETTING STARTED

Permanent Desktop Items
*System folders have special functions and cannot be removed
from the desktop.*

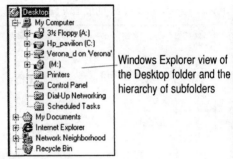

Windows Explorer view of
the Desktop folder and the
hierarchy of subfolders

 My Computer

A system folder that contains all the drives your computer is
connected to, as well as system folders such as **Control Panel**
and **Printers**. *See My Computer, page 22.*

 Network Neighborhood

A system folder that indicates your ability to connect to a
network. It contains icons that allow you to browse resources
on other computers to which your computer is connected. *See
Browse Network Computers, page 207.*

 Recycle Bin

A system folder that stores the items you "delete." Items in the
Recycle Bin can be restored or permanently deleted at a later
time. *See The Recycle Bin, page 25.*

GETTING STARTED

Other Desktop Items

 Internet Explorer

An icon that starts Internet Explorer when clicked, or starts the **Internet Connection Wizard** to guide you through the steps to set up an Internet connection. *See Internet Explorer, page 185.*

 Channels Bar

A bar that contains links to enriched Web content that is "pushed" (delivered in a stream) to your computer when you select a channel. Channel content is viewed through Microsoft Internet Explorer. *See Use Channels, page 69.*

 **Taskbar**

A bar that contains the **Start** button, optional toolbars, and the notification area (the right-most area that contains system icons, such as the clock and volume control). Applications that are running will also appear on the taskbar. The taskbar is placed at the bottom of the desktop by default. The taskbar may be moved to any position on the desktop, and its size can also be changed. *See The Taskbar, page 27, and Change Taskbar and Start Menu Appearance, page 101.*

GETTING STARTED

Items You Can Add to the Desktop

Shortcuts to Applications

You can create shortcuts to applications you run often and place them on the desktop. A shortcut is identified by the jump arrow in the bottom left corner of the shortcut icon. *See Create Shortcuts, page 96.*

Shortcuts to Folders

You can create shortcuts to folders you open often. A shortcut is identified by the jump arrow in the bottom left corner of the shortcut icon. *See Create Shortcuts, page 96.*

Folders

You can create folders directly on the desktop. *See Work with Folders and Files, page 164.* You can also create shortcuts to network folders and drives. Folders store related items, such as files and other folders.

In previous versions of Windows, folders were referred to as directories.

Files

You can create files directly on the desktop (*see Work with Folders and Files, page 164*) or save files to the desktop folder when using an application (*see Save Files from Windows Application, page 169*).

GETTING STARTED

CONTROL PANEL

*From the **Control Panel** you can change a wide range of computer settings. You can access Control Panel from the **Start** menu, or from the **My Computer** folder. Additional icons may appear in your **Control Panel** window depending on the applications and devices you have installed on your computer.*

Open Control Panel

You can view or change settings for a variety of devices and applications installed on your computer.

☞ *From the Start Menu*

1 Click **Start** .... 📖

2 Point to **Settings** .... 🗂 Settings

3 Click **Control Panel** .... 🖥 Control Panel

*The **Control Panel** window opens.*

4 Click icons for the settings you want to change.

☞ *From the My Computer Folder*

1 Click **My Computer** icon .... 💻 My Computer
on the desktop.

2 Click **Control Panel** icon .... 🖥 Control Panel
in the **My Computer** window.

*The **Control Panel** window opens.*

3 Click icons for the settings you want to change.

Getting Started

DIALOG BOX CONTROLS

When you select certain commands, a dialog box will open displaying related options. Some dialog boxes contain named tabs that you can click to display additional options.

Open a Dialog Box

> 📖 *Menu commands that open a dialog box will be followed by ellipsis marks (...).*

1 Click desired menu name.......................**Alt** +*underlined letter*

2 Click desired command ....*underlined letter*
   on drop-down menu that appears.

   To close dialog box and cancel changes:

   • Click **Cancel** command button ....**Esc**

Move Within a Dialog Box

   • Move forward...**Tab**
   OR
   Move backward ....**Shift** + **Tab**

Use Dialog Box Components

Dialog boxes contain controls that provide different ways for you to specify a setting or choose an option:

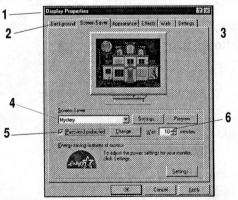

GETTING STARTED

✓ *Click the **Apply** button to try out new settings without closing the dialog box.*

❶ title bar

The title bar identifies the title of the dialog box. Drag it to move the dialog box to another area. Do this to view data behind the dialog box.

❷ tab

Named tabs display options related to the name in the same dialog box. Click to access its options.

To move through dialog box tabs:

- Move forward...`Ctrl` + `Tab`

OR

Move backward..`Ctrl` + `Shift` + `Tab`

❸ Help button

Click the button, then click the option or element you want help with, to view a description of the setting. When you click the **Help** button, the pointer becomes an arrow with a question mark. *See **Basic Mouse Skills**, page 4.*

❹ drop-down list

Click a drop-down list to open a short list of options, then make a choice from options provided. You can click any area on a drop-down list box to open it.

To select drop-down list box item:

1 Click desired drop-down list box...`Tab`

2 Highlight desired item ....`↑` `↓`

continued...

GETTING STARTED

Use Dialog Box Components (cont.)

❺ check box

A check mark in the box indicates the option is selected.
If several check boxes are offered, you may select more than one. Click to select or deselect option.

To select/deselect check box:

1   Move to check box beside desired item .... `Tab`

2   Click to select or deselect desired item .... `Space`

❻ spin box (increment box)

Type value in the box, or click up or down arrow
(usually to right of box) to select value.

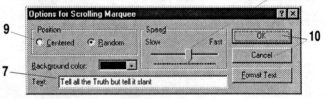

❼ text box

A text box is a space where you can type information.
Click in the text box and type desired information, or select
existing information in text box and type over it to replace it.

To type information in a text box:

1   Click desired text box .... `Tab`

2   Type desired information .... *data*

To replace existing information in a text box:

1   Double-click in desired text box.

    OR

    Drag through data in text box to select it.

2   Type over selection.

❽ slider

Drag to increase or decrease value for a setting.

18

GETTING STARTED

Use Dialog Box Components (cont.)

❾ option buttons (radio buttons)

A selected option button contains a dark circle. You may choose only one option in a set of option buttons. Click to select one option appearing in a set of options.

To select option button:

1 Move to option button area...Tab

2 Click hollow circle beside desired item ....

❿ command button

Click the desired button to execute its command.

FOLDERS AND FILES

Folders store related items such as files and other folders. Please note that in previous versions of Windows, folders were called directories. Files are items that store information, such as the data you create when using an application. See Folders and Files, page 130.

 Icons represent files and folders. When you click a file or folder icon, Windows opens it.

System Folders

The system folders described below are special folders that Windows maintains for specific purposes. System folders cannot be moved to another folder or deleted.

 The Desktop

All other folders can be accessed from this root folder. When you first start Windows, the desktop folder is presented as the screen background. The desktop appears just as other folders when you view it from **Windows Explorer** or from an **Open** or **Save** dialog box when using Windows 98 applications. *See The Desktop, page 11.*

continued...

GETTING STARTED

System Folders (cont.)

 My Computer

This folder contains your computer's drive icons and the **Control Panel, Printers, Dial-Up Networking,** and **Scheduled Tasks** system folders. *See My Computer, page 22.*

 Internet Explorer

When you open this folder/browser, Windows will dial up and connect to the Internet if you have an account with an Internet provider. It will then allow you to browse Internet sites. *See Internet Tools, page 177.*

 Network Neighborhood

This system folder indicates your ability to connect to a network. It may contain computer icons (network computers) that you can browse to view or use shared resources such as folders and printers. *See Browse Network Computers, page 207.*

 Recycle Bin

This folder stores the files and folders you "delete." *See The Recycle Bin, page 25.*

Other Folders and Files

Windows provides additional folders that you can use to store other folders and files. (See Special Folders, page 160.) You can also create your own folders in which to store subfolders and files. You can create folders anywhere except in system folders like My Computer or Recycle Bin. You can create folders directly on the desktop. See Work with Folders and Files, page 164.

Personal Folders

For example, you can create a folder named Art in which to store graphic files. You could then organize the contents of the Art folder by creating subfolders within Art, such as Animals.

FILE TYPES

You can tell a document's file type and the application it is associated with by the file extension. See Change File Types, page 175.

Folder and File Paths

A path is a notation used to identify the location of a folder or file, such as C:\my docs\art.

SET WINDOWS TO DISPLAY FULL PATH NAME

You can set Windows to display the full path of a folder in the window's title bar.

1 Click **Start** .... 📖

2 Point to **Settings** .... 🔧 Settings

3 Click **Folder Options** .... 📋 Folder Options...

4 Click **View** tab .... Ctrl + Tab

5 Select **Display the full path in title bar** check box.

6 Click **OK** .... Enter

GETTING STARTED

Naming Folders and Files

File names may contain spaces and can be as long as 255 characters.
*They cannot, however, contain the following characters: \ * ? " < > |*

Windows creates an alias for each long file name so programs written
for versions of Windows prior to Windows 95 can read the new files.
For example, the file name MY FIRST DRAFT.TXT would appear as
MYFIRS~1.TXT in these programs.

MY COMPUTER

My Computer is a system folder that appears on the desktop. It
contains disk drive and system folder icons. You can use the My
Computer folder as a starting point to browse all the drives connected
to your computer, including network drives that have been mapped
(assigned a drive letter).

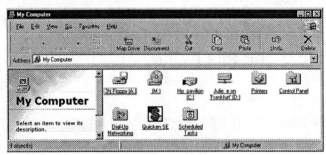

Open My Computer

⌧ Without the Desktop Displayed

1 Click  on taskbar to view desktop.

2 Click **My Computer** icon.. 🖳

⌧ With the Desktop Displayed

▪ Click **My Computer** icon.. 🖳

GETTING STARTED

Open My Computer (cont.)

⌕ From Any Folder Window

- Select **My Computer** from hierarchy of folders in **Address bar** list box.

⌕ From Windows Explorer

- Select **My Computer** from hierarchy of folders in **All Folders** pane.

⌕ From an Open, Save or Find Dialog Box

- Select **My Computer** from the **Look in** or **Save in** list box.

GETTING STARTED

My Computer Icons

*Icons represent objects in your computer system. If a file icon is associated with an application (it's a registered file type), you can click or double-click the file to open it into its application in one step. In the Classic viewing style, when you double-click an icon, a new window opens displaying its contents. Icons in this list, however, are in the Web browsing style. Underlined icons indicate that Web browsing is in effect, and icons need only be clicked once. See **The Active Desktop**, page 74 and **Change Folder Browsing Style**, page 133.*

Click icon: To:

Display contents of floppy disk.

Display contents of hard disk.

Display contents of shared hard disk.

Display contents of CD-ROM.

Display contents of network drive, if you are part of a network and you have mapped a connection to one.

Control Panel

Open **Control Panel** folder to change system settings.

Printers

Open **Printers** folder to set up or manage printers and printer queues.

Dial-Up Networking

Open **Dial-Up Networking** folder to set up or manage dial-up connections to other computers.

Scheduled Tasks

Open **Scheduled Tasks** folder to set up or manage tasks scheduled to run at specific times.

The following icons are available when you browse drive icons:

Open folder.

Open shared folder.

Open file.

GETTING STARTED

THE RECYCLE BIN

*The **Recycle Bin** is a system folder in which Windows stores the files and folders you delete.*

Recycle Bin Features

- Items you drag onto the **Recycle Bin** icon are stored there until you remove them, or until they take up a specified percentage of available hard disk space.

- If you delete an item by pressing ▨Delete▨, Windows sometimes places it in the Recycle Bin.

- You can restore all items (or just selected ones) in the Recycle Bin to their original locations.

  💣 *Sometimes deleted items are not sent to the Recycle Bin. Items deleted from floppy disks or network drives are permanently deleted. Items deleted through applications from an MS-DOS command prompt are also permanently deleted.*

- You cannot restore files that you "empty" from the Recycle Bin; they are permanently deleted.

- You can empty all items (or just selected ones) in the Recycle Bin. Doing this will permanently delete the items.

  💣 *If you delete an entire folder, all of the folder's contents are placed in the Recycle Bin, including its subfolders.*

The Recycle Bin Icon

*The appearance of the **Recycle Bin** icon tells you whether or not it is empty:*

Recycle Bin
(full)   Recycle Bin
             (empty)

GETTING STARTED

OPEN RECYCLE BIN

- Click **Recycle Bin** icon...

CHANGE RECYCLE BIN PROPERTIES

1 Right-click **Recycle Bin** icon...

2 Click **Properties** on shortcut menu................................. Ⓡ

DELETE ITEMS PERMENANTLY

        ☞ Using SHIFT Key

- Press **Shift** while dragging item onto Recycle Bin..........

  OR

  Press **Shift** while pressing **Delete**........................... **Shift** + **Delete**

   💣 *The above procedure is not reversible.*

        ☞ Using the Recycle Bin Icon

1 Right-click **Recycle Bin** icon...

2 Click **Empty Recycle Bin**.. Ⓑ

        ☞ From the Recycle Bin Window

1 Click **File** menu... Ⓕ

2 Click **Empty Recycle Bin**.. Ⓑ

3 Click ▢Yes or ▢No as desired.. Ⓨ/Ⓝ

GETTING STARTED

THE TASKBAR

*When you start Windows 98 for the first time, the taskbar appears at the bottom of the screen. The **Start** button is located on the far left side of the taskbar and the notification area is on the far right. Folders and applications appear as buttons on the taskbar when you open them. A new feature of Windows 98 is the inclusion of toolbars on the taskbar.*

Taskbar Features

The primary purpose of the taskbar is to make it easy for you to switch between or start new tasks. As you open more folders and applications, the buttons that appear on the taskbar will get smaller to make room for any additional buttons. If, however, more folders or applications are opened than can be displayed, scroll arrows will appear on the taskbar so that you can click to bring the desired taskbar button(s) into view.

—— scroll arrows

The taskbar's many features include:

- *Easy access to the **Start** button. See **The Start Menu**, page 8.*

- *Easy access to features installed as tools on the **taskbar** toolbar. See **Customize Taskbar Toolbars**, page 108.*

- *Easy access to folders and applications displayed as **taskbar** buttons. See **Switch Tasks**, page 60.*

Use the Taskbar

- Click any application or folder button that appears on taskbar to quickly restore or minimize it. *See **Window Controls**, page 30.*

- Right-click taskbar to arrange or minimize windows of open items and select from options on a **shortcut** menu. *See **Window Controls**, page 30.*

continued...

GETTING STARTED

Use Taskbar (cont.)

- Read settings that appear in notification area (such as system time). When your modem is active or while you are printing, icons for these processes appear in the notification area. You can also access devices and programs that appear in this area by double-clicking them.

- Drag taskbar or its edges to change its size or position.

- Right-click taskbar, click **Properties** on shortcut menu to select special options. For example, you can choose to automatically hide the taskbar. *See **Change Taskbar and Start Menu Appearance**, page 101.*

IDENTIFY TASKBAR ITEMS

- Point to desired item.

  Windows displays the name of the item in a box.

Quick Launch Toolbar

CONTROL PROGRAMS FROM TASKBAR

✓ *Press the* ⊞ *key and* Tab *simultaneously in order to cycle through buttons on the taskbar.*

1 Right-click desired program button on taskbar.

2 Click desired control command on shortcut menu:

- **R**estore .... R
- **M**ove .... M
- **S**ize .... S
- Mi**n**imize .... N
- Ma**x**imize X
- **C**lose.. C

SIZE TASKBAR

The taskbar changes to accommodate items that appear on it.

SIZE TASKBAR VERTICALLY USING MOUSE

1 Point to top of taskbar.

The pointer becomes a ↕

2 Drag sizing arrow in direction you want to size the taskbar.

SIZE TASKBAR VERTICALLY USING KEYBOARD

1 Select taskbar .... `Ctrl` + `Esc` , `Esc` , `Tab`

2 Right-click to open shortcut menu .... `Alt` + `Space`

3 Click **Size** .... `S`

A ✛ appears in the middle of the taskbar.

4 Increase taskbar to desired size .... `↑`

OR

Decrease taskbar to desired size .... `↓`

5 Press **Enter** .... `Enter`

SIZE AND MOVE AREAS ON THE TASKBAR

1 Point to slide bar on taskbar.

slide bar ———

The pointer becomes a ↔

2 Drag slide bar in desired direction to move or size task area.

> ✓ *If you drag the left sizing bar completely over an area, the areas will switch positions on the taskbar.*

GETTING STARTED

HIDE TASKBAR

☞ *From the Desktop*

1 Point to top of taskbar.

The pointer becomes a ↕

2 Drag sizing arrow down until taskbar is hidden from view.

☞ *From the Start Menu*

1 Click **Start** .... 🏁

2 Point to **Settings** .... 🗂 Settings

3 Click **Taskbar & Start Menu** .... 📑 Taskbar & Start Menu...

4 Select **Auto hide** check box .... Alt + U

5 Click **OK** .... Enter

WINDOW CONTROLS

You can use graphical elements such as window borders, title bars, and close buttons to control the size and position of folder and application windows. Window controls are utilized by clicking or dragging the mouse.

> 📖 *When you rest the mouse pointer on a window control button, such as the **Maximize** button, Windows displays its name.*

Use Window Controls

Click button:	To:
❎ **Close**	Close window.
◻ **Maximize**	Enlarge window to fill screen.
➖ **Minimize**	Reduce window to button on taskbar. When working with document windows, click to reduce the window to a button within the application window.
🔲 **Restore**	Restore maximized window to its previous size.

GETTING STARTED

Window Controls (cont.)

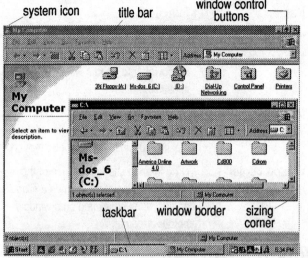

system icon   title bar   window control buttons

taskbar   window border   sizing corner

📖 *In the illustration above, the **My Computer** window contains **Close, Restore,** and **Minimize** buttons, while the **C:\ folder** window contains the **Close, Maximize,** and **Minimize** buttons. Unlike the maximized **My Computer** window, you can size and move the **C:\ folder** window because it has not been maximized.*

Name:	Function:
sizing pointer	The mouse pointer becomes a sizing pointer when you rest it on a window border or corner. This change indicates that you can size the window by dragging its border.
system icon	Click to open the system menu.
window control buttons	Click to open a menu of commands that control the window (e.g., **Restore, Mi**_n_**imize,** and **C**_l_**ose**).

continued...

31

Getting Started

Window Controls (cont.)

Name:	Function:
taskbar	Click taskbar buttons to select a window that is not in view (hidden behind other windows) or to open a window you have minimized.
title bar	Drag it to move a window, or double-click it to maximize/restore the window. Maximized windows cannot be moved.
window border and sizing corner	Drag them to change the size of the window. The pointer becomes a sizing pointer when positioned on a window border or corner.

Work with Windows

*The **active window** is displayed in front of all other windows, and its button is highlighted on the taskbar. Select any open window by clicking its button on the taskbar. Click the **Desktop** button on the **Quick Launch** taskbar toolbar to minimize all windows and view the desktop.*

*Each window has a **system menu** button in the upper-left corner that you can click to select window commands from a menu. You can also control windows by right-clicking the application or folder button on the taskbar and clicking the desired option on the menu that appears.*

OPEN SYSTEM MENU

- Click system icon in top left corner of window.

  OR

  Click application or folder window .... +

SIZE WINDOW

SIZE WINDOW USING MOUSE

1 Point to border or corner of window to size.

The pointer becomes a ↕

2 Drag window border in desired direction.

SIZE WINDOWS USING KEYBOARD

1 Select desired open window .... `Alt` + `Tab`

> ✓ *Holding down* `Alt` *while pressing* `Tab` *will let you scroll through open windows.*

2 Open **System** menu .... `Alt` + `Space`

3 Click **Size** .... `S`

The pointer becomes a ✛

4 Choose border to size by pressing corresponding key only once.

5 Move pointer until desired size is obtained.

6 Press **Enter** .... `Enter`

MOVE WINDOW

- Drag title bar of window in desired direction.

OR

1 Select desired window .... `Alt` + `Tab`

2 Open **System** menu .... `Alt` + `Space`

3 Click **Move** .... `M`

The pointer becomes a ✛

4 Move pointer in desired direction.

5 Press **Enter** .... `Enter`

GETTING STARTED

SHOW WINDOW CONTENTS WHILE MOVING WINDOW

1 Click **Start** .... 🔳

2 Point to **Settings** .... 🔳 Settings

3 Click **Folder Options** .... 🔳 Folder Options...

4 Click **View** tab .... **Ctrl** + **Tab**

5 Select **Show window contents while dragging** check box.

6 Click **OK**

MINIMIZE WINDOW

- Click the window's **Minimize** button .... 🔳

OR

1 Open **System** menu .... **Alt** + **Space**

2 Click **Minimize** .... **N**

MAXIMIZE WINDOW

- Click the window's **Maximize** button .... 🔳

OR

1 Open the **System** menu .... **Alt** + **Space**

2 Click **Maximize** .... **X**

> 📖 *After maximizing a window, the **Maximize** button
> becomes a **Restore** button.*

RESTORE MAXIMIZED WINDOW

- Click the window's **Restore** button .... 🔳

OR

1 Open **System** menu .... **Alt** + **Space**

GETTING STARTED

Restore Window (cont.)

2 Click **Restore**..

After restoring a window, the Restore button becomes a Maximize button.

> ✓ *You can also restore and maximize a particular window by double-clicking the window title bar. You can also restore and minimize a particular window by clicking its taskbar button.*

MINIMIZE ALL WINDOWS

- Press the **Windows** key and **M** ....

RESTORE ALL WINDOWS

- Press the **Windows** key and **D**......................................

UNDO MINIMIZE ALL WINDOWS

- Press the **Windows** key, **Shift** and **M** ....

SCROLL THROUGH A WINDOW

☞ Using Scroll Arrows

- Click left or right scroll arrow to scroll horizontally in small steps through list or workspace.

OR

Click up or down scroll arrow to scroll vertically in small steps through list or workspace.

☞ Using Scroll Box

- Drag horizontal scroll box to scroll horizontally to any position in list or workspace.

OR

Drag vertical scroll box to scroll vertically to any position in list or workspace.

continued...

GETTING STARTED

Scroll Through Window (cont.)

☞ Using Scroll Bar

- Click vertical scroll bar above or below scroll box to move vertically to previous or next area in list or workspace.

OR

- Click horizontal scroll bar to right or left of scroll box to move horizontally to previous or next area in list or workspace.

SELECT OTHER WINDOWS (SWITCH TASKS)

- Click previously used window ....

OR

Switch to another window by holding down **Alt** while repeatedly pressing **Tab**.

OR

Click other window's button on taskbar.

CLOSE A WINDOW

- Click window's **Close** button..

OR

1 Open **System** menu ....

2 Click **Close** ....

To quickly close an application or folder window:

- Press **Alt** while pressing **F4** ....

CLOSE CURRENT FOLDER AND ALL PARENT WINDOWS

- Press **Shift** and click window **Close** button ....

GETTING STARTED

GETTING HELP

Windows 98 provides online **Help** *so that you can look up how to perform a procedure or you can obtain additional information about what you see in a dialog box. The* **Windows Help** *window contains three tabs:* **Contents, Index,** *and* **Search.**

Tabs

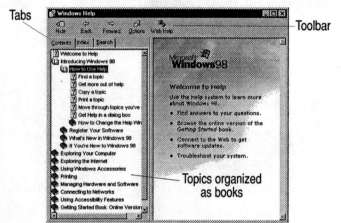

Toolbar

Topics organized as books

Open Help Quickly

- Press **Windows** key and **F1** simultaneously ....

OPEN HELP CONTENTS TAB

The **Contents** *tab displays Windows Help organized like a table of contents in a book.*

1 Click ![Start]

2 Click **Help** ....

3 Click **Contents** tab, if necessary .... Alt + C

GETTING STARTED

DISPLAY HELP CONTENTS

1 Click closed topic (book) to open it ....

Additional books or content items appear.

2 Click second-level book ....

if necessary, to open its contents.

> ✓ *If you open the wrong topic, click the open book icon again* 📖 *to close it.*

3 Click desired content item .... ❓

to view it in the right pane.

> ✓ *You can click* 🔲 *on the* **Windows Help** *toolbar to*
> *hide the left pane. When you do this,* 🔲 *becomes*
> 🔲*, and the entire* **Help** *window displays informa-*
> *tion for the selected Help item.*

The Index Tab

The **Index** *tab lists Help items alphabetically like an index in a book.*

FIND HELP USING INDEX TAB

1 Click 🔲 Start .... 📖

2 Click **Help** .... 📖 Help

3 Click **Index** tab .... Alt + I

4 Type part or all of the word(s) ....*word(s)*
you are looking for.

Windows selects items automatically as you type.

OR

Browse Help items in list by using scroll bar to scroll list.

GETTING STARTED

Find Help Using Index Tab (cont.)

5 Double-click desired **Help** menu .... ⬆️ ⬇️ Enter

to open it.

OR

Click [Display] .... Alt + D

to show help for the selected item.

*An additional window may appear displaying multiple Help items
for your selection. Double-click the desired item to continue.*

> ✓ *Click* [Back] *and* [Forward] *to move through the Help
> content you've seen.*

The Search Tab

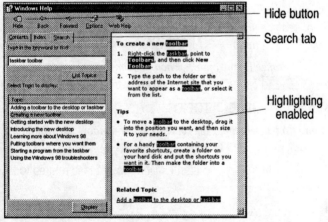
— Hide button
— Search tab
— Highlighting enabled

*The **Search** tab lets you search for references to word(s) you type in
all Help topics.*

SEARCH FOR HELP ITEMS

1 Click [Start] .... 📖

2 Click **Help** .... Help

3 Click **Search** tab.. Alt + S

continued...

Getting Started

Search for Help Items (cont.)

4 Type the word(s) you wish to find.....................................*word(s)*
in the text box.

You can type a phrase to narrow the focus of your search.

5 Click `List Topics` .... `Alt`+`L`

Help information appears in the list.

6 Double-click desired item in the list.

OR

Click `Display` .... `Alt`+`D`

to show help for the selected item.

Help Options

*After you find a Help topic, the window may contain links to other
topics. When you are changing settings in a dialog box, you can also
find the help you need.*

*You can minimize Help windows when you continue to work. You can
click* `Windows Help` *on the taskbar to maximize the* **Help** *window again.*

JUMP TO OTHER HELP TOPICS

*After you find a Help topic, the contents of the window may contain
links to other topics and Windows processes.*

- Click `Click here` (a link) to start a Windows process related to the
Help topic.

OR

Click `Related Topics` to view related Help topics.

OR

Click `Back` or `Forward` to display Help topics you have
already seen.

OR

Click `Web Help` on the **Help** toolbar to access Online Help.

USE HELP TOPIC OPTIONS

1 Click [Options] on **Help** toolbar .... `Alt`+`O`

2 Click desired Help option:

- **Hide** **T**abs .... `T`

  *removes tabs and the left frame from view to increase
  display space. After selecting this option, select Show Tabs
  from the same menu to view tabs and left frame again.*

- **B**ack .... `B`

  views previous Help topic.

- **F**orward .... `F`

  views next Help topic.

- **S**top .... `S`

  stops last action.

- **R**efresh .... `R`

  reloads display of current Help topic.

- **W**eb Help .... `W`

  accesses Support Online Help.

- **C**ustomize .... `C`

  *changes colors and fonts in the right pane of the
  Help window.*

- **P**rint .... `P`

  prints the current Help topic.

- Highlighting **O**n/Off .... `O`

  *highlights the keyword(s) found when using the Search
  tab. You can turn this option off by selecting Highlighting
  Off from the same menu.*

GETTING STARTED

Get Help in a Dialog Box

1 Click **Help** button...🔲

The pointer becomes a ⌖?

2 Click the item you want help with.

A pop-up window appears with a description of the setting.

KEYBOARD SHORTCUTS

Keyboard shortcuts sometimes provide faster ways of accomplishing tasks. This Quick Reference Guide provides you with keyboard shortcuts whenever possible.

Look Up Keyboard Shortcuts

1 Click **Start** ....🏴

2 Click **Help** ....📖 Help

3 Click **Index** tab ....**Alt**+**I**

4 Type *keyboard shortcuts* in the provided text box.

✓ *If you use a **Windows 95-ready keyboard** or a compatible keyboard, you can use the **Windows key** 🏴 to perform many tasks.*

WINDOWS ACCESSORIES

Windows 98 comes with an array of accessories that can help you manage your system, entertain you, and help you to do your work.

This Accessory:	Lets you:
🖮 Accessibility	Access tools to change keyboard, sound, display, and mouse behavior for people with mobility, hearing, or visual impairments.
🖫 Backup	Back up files to a local, network, or tape drive.

GETTING STARTED

Windows Accessories (cont.)

Calculator	Perform calculations.
CD Player	Play audio and compact discs.
Character Map	Select and insert special characters into any Windows document.
Clipboard Viewer	View data stored in the Clipboard.
Dial-Up Networking	Connect to local and network resources on a remote computer that is running Dial-Up server software.
Direct Cable Connection	Connect to the local and network resources on a Windows computer that is also running Direct Cable Connection.
Disk Cleanup	Free up space on your hard drive.
Disk Defragmenter	Rearrange files and unused space on your hard disk so that programs run faster.
DriveSpace	Compress files on a disk; provides commands to manage compressed disks.
Games	Play FreeCell, Hearts, Minesweeper, and Solitaire games.
HyperTerminal	Connect to a remote computer to exchange information and files.
Imaging	View, annotate, and perform basic tasks with image documents, including fax documents and scanned images.
Maintenance Wizard	Employ Start Up options to improve Windows start time, schedule Disk Defragmenter and ScanDisk to maintain disk speed and reliability, and schedule deletion of unnecessary files.

continued...

GETTING STARTED

Windows Accessories (cont.)

Media Player	Play multimedia files, such as video files and compact disks.
Microsoft FrontPage Express	Edit an HTML page.
Microsoft NetMeeting	Call people on the Internet or a LAN in order to hold digital conversations, share applications, draw on a shared white board, and send files and messages.
Microsoft NetShow Player	View live TV/radio-like broadcasts from the Internet and/or your corporate intranet, and view local or network-based stored content.
The Microsoft Network	Access Microsoft's online information service.
Microsoft Wallet	Store private information in a secure place for Internet shopping.
My Briefcase	Synchronize files you work with on different computers.
Net Watcher	Monitor, manage, and create network shares on your computer and administer network shares on a remote computer.
Notepad	Create and edit text files.
Outlook Express	Access e-mail and newsgroup services, use multiple mail accounts, and store and retrieve e-mail addresses.
Paint	Create, edit, and display bitmap images.
Personal Web Server	Serve Web pages directly from your desktop Web site.
Phone Dialer	Record and dial phone numbers from your computer.

Windows Accessories (cont.)

Quick View	Preview a document without opening it.
Real Audio Player	Access Live and On-Demand audio, video, and animation from the Internet.
ScanDisk	Scan and fix errors found on disks.
Sound Recorder	Record, play back, and edit sounds.
System Information	Allow a technical support representative to diagnose your computer system trouble more quickly and efficiently. Contains system tools you can use to maintain Windows 98.
Volume Control	Control the audio volume for playback, recording, and other installed audio devices.
Web Publishing Wizard	Upload Web page content easily to a Web server.
Web-Based Enterprise Mgmt	Develop applications for remote management of computer hardware and software.
WebTV for Windows	Display both standard and interactive television broadcasts.
Welcome To Windows	Tour the Windows 98 operating system features with a multimedia presentation.
Windows Update	Download the latest drivers and Windows components to help keep your system up to date.
WordPad	Create, edit, format, and print documents.

Consult the Windows 98 online Help for instructions on how to use these utilities.

APPLICATIONS

ABOUT APPLICATIONS

Applications are special files that contain code, or program instructions, that the computer carries out when you open them. You will run an application so that you can perform a task, such as word processing, accounting, or browsing the Internet.

Windows 98 makes it easy to run and manage your applications by offering the following capabilities:

- *Add and remove applications from your computer.*
- *Launch and exit applications.*
- *Manage multiple applications.*
- *Transfer and paste data and objects from one running application to another.*

ADD OR REMOVE APPLICATIONS
The Add/Remove Programs Tool

*The **Add/Remove Programs** tool makes the task of installing applications easy. With this tool, you just click the **Install** command button and Windows 98 automatically searches for the installation program in your floppy or CD-ROM drive.*

1 Click **Start** ....

2 Point to **Settings**... **Settings**

3 Click **Control Panel** .... **Control Panel**

4 Click **Add/Remove Programs** icon .... Add/Remove Programs

   *The **Add/Remove Programs Properties** dialog box appears.*

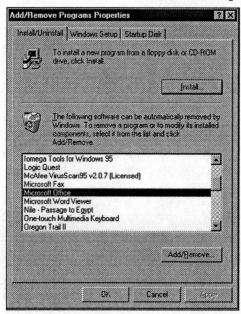

5 Click **Install/Uninstall** tab...................................... Ctrl + Tab
if necessary.

6 Click Install.. Alt + I

*The Install Program From Floppy Disk or CD-Rom
dialog box appears.*

7 Insert setup CD-ROM or disk for new application.

8 Click Next > when prompted .... Alt + N

*Windows searches all floppy and CD-ROM disk drives
for program installation files.*

📖 *If Windows 98 finds the wrong installation files, you
can find the correct files yourself by browsing your
computer system. See **Use the Browse Button**, page 146.*

continued...

Applications

Add/Remove Programs (cont.)

9 Click [Finish] when prompted ....

10 Follow application setup prompts.

*After you install a Windows application, Windows 98 auto-matically creates a shortcut to the program in the **Programs** menu so you can run the application from the **Start** menu.*

Add Applications Using Run Command

*If you know the location and name of the installation file, you can use the **Run** command, rather than the **Add/Remove Programs** tool, to install a program.*

1 Click [Start] ....

2 Click **R**un ....

*The **Run** dialog box appears.*

3 Type installation program path and filename ....*path\name* (e.g., *a:\setup*).

OR

Click [Browse...] .... [Alt] + [B]

to locate and select the application to add. *See **Use the Browse Button**, page 146.*

4 Click [OK] .... [Enter]

Windows 98 will run the setup file.

5 Follow setup prompts for application.

*After you install a Windows application, Windows 98 automatically creates a shortcut to the program in the **Programs** menu so you can run the application from the **Start** menu.*

Remove Applications from Your Computer

*You can remove many Windows applications from the **Add/Remove Programs Properties** dialog box. When you remove applications in this way, you can be certain that the application and all related files are deleted from your hard disk.*

This procedure, however, only removes applications designed for use with Windows versions 95 and 98. You may not be able to remove MS-DOS applications and older Windows applications with this procedure. In such cases, consult the documentation that came with the application you want to delete.

1 Click **Start**

2 Point to **Settings** .... Settings

3 Click **Control Panel** .... Control Panel

4 Click **Add/Remove Programs** icon .... Add/Remove Programs

   *The **Add/Remove Programs Properties** dialog box appears.*

5 Click **Install/Uninstall** tab .... Ctrl + Tab
   if necessary.

6 Select program to remove from list box.

   📖 *If the application you want to remove does not appear in the list, consult the application documentation for instructions on how to uninstall the program.*

7 Click Add/Remove.. .... Alt + R

8 Click Yes .... Y
   when uninstall confirmation box appears.

9 Follow on-screen prompts.

   Windows 98 removes the application.

   📖 *You may need to insert the program CD-ROM or selected floppy disks to complete the program removal.*

Applications

Add or Remove Windows Components

You can add or remove accessory applications that were installed with the Windows 98 operating system.

⚒ *From Control Panel*

1 Click **Start** ....

2 Point to **Settings** .... **Settings**

3 Click **Control Panel** .... **Control Panel**

4 Click **Add/Remove Programs** icon .... Add/Remove Programs

*The **Add/Remove Programs Properties** dialog box appears.*

5 Click **Windows Setup** tab .... **Ctrl** + **Tab**

To add an entire component:

- Select check box next to component(s) you want to add in **Components** list box.

A check mark appears next to the desired component(s).

To remove an entire component:

- Select check box next to component you want to remove in **Components** list box.

The check mark next to the unwanted component disappears.

To add/remove parts of a component:

a Click component name in **Components** list box.

b Click **Details...** .... **Alt** + **D**

c Select/deselect check box(es) for component feature(s) that you want to add or remove.

d Click **OK** .... **Enter**
  to return to the **Windows Setup** tab.

The check box next to the modified component becomes shaded to indicate that only part of its features have been selected.

e Click `Apply` .... `Alt` + `A`

*If prompted, insert the CD-ROM or floppy disks as
requested and follow any additional on-screen instructions.*

USE APPLICATION SHORTCUTS

*Windows 98 lets you place shortcuts to run an application directly on
the desktop and on the Start menu. You can also assign keyboard
shortcuts to start applications quickly.*

Add Application Shortcut to Start Menu

*A **shortcut** is an icon that, when clicked, links directly to an application or file. By default, shortcuts to programs (applications) are stored
in the **Programs** folder of the **Start** menu. However, you can add
shortcuts to frequently used applications to the **Start** menu. See **Add
Items to Start Menu**, page 103.*

1 Click `Start` ....

2 Point to **Settings** .... `Settings`

3 Click **Taskbar & Start Menu** .... `Taskbar & Start Menu...`

*The **Taskbar Properties** dialog box appears.*

4 Click **Start Menu Programs** tab .... `Ctrl` + `Tab`

5 Click `Add...` .... `Alt` + `A`

*The **Create Shortcut** dialog box appears.*

6 Type application file path...*path*
in the **Command** line (e.g., *c:\wp\wp.exe*).

OR

Click `Browse...` .... `Alt` + `R`

to locate and select the application file on your hard drive.
*See **Use the Browse Button**, page 146.*

7 Click `Next >` .... `Alt` + `N`

continued...

APPLICATIONS

Add Shortcut to Start Menu (cont.)

8 Select **Start Menu Folder** .... ⬆️ ⬇️

> 📖 *To create a new folder, select parent folder, click **New Folder** button, then type desired name.*

9 Click [Next >] .... Alt + N

10 Type shortcut name...*name*

You can use the Windows 98 default name for the shortcut.

11 Click [Finish] .... Enter

12 Click [OK] .... Enter

to close **Taskbar Properties** dialog box.

Remove Application Shortcut from Start Menu

You can delete a shortcut to an application without deleting the application from the hard disk.

1 Click [🪟 Start] .... 📇

2 Point to **Settings**.. 🖥️ Settings

3 Click **Taskbar & Start Menu** .... 🪟 Taskbar & Start Menu...

4 Click **Start Menu Programs** tab .... Ctrl + Tab
if necessary.

5 Click [Remove...] .... Alt + R

*The **Remove Shortcuts/Folders** dialog box appears.*

6 Select item you want to remove....................... ⬆️ ⬇️ ➡️ ⬅️

7 Click [Remove...] .... Alt + R

8 Click [Close] .... Enter

9 Click [OK] .... Enter

> 📖 *The **Advanced** button takes you directly to Windows Explorer.*

Create Keyboard Shortcuts to Open Applications or Folders

You can add an application shortcut to your desktop. See **Create Shortcuts,** *page 96. You can then assign a keystroke to start the application.*

1 Right-click application or application shortcut icon.

2 Click **Properties** .... $\boxed{R}$

The application or icon's **Properties** *dialog box appears.*

3 Click in **Shortcut key** box .... $\boxed{Alt}$ + $\boxed{K}$

4 Press desired key to use for shortcut.

5 Click ▐ OK ▐ .... $\boxed{Enter}$

OPEN AND EXIT APPLICATIONS

You can open applications by using the **Start** *menu, by opening associated documents, or by using the* **Run** *command.*

Open Applications Using Start Menu

1 Click ▐ Start ▐ ....

2 Point to **Programs** ....

The **Programs** *menu appears.*

3 Click program you want to run on submenu that appears.
OR
If desired application is in subfolder, point to that subfolder and click desired program on submenu that appears.

The program will run and a taskbar button with the application name will appear.

> 📖 *Each application you run requires part of the system's memory. Available memory is reduced each time you open an additional application. This can result in system slow-downs if you do not have enough memory installed.*

APPLICATIONS

Open Windows Component Applications

You can open Windows 98 component applications, such as WordPad and Calculator, from the Start menu.

1 Click **Start** .... 📕

2 Point to **Programs** .... 🔲 Programs

3 Point to **Accessories** .... 📓 Accessories

The Windows 98 Accessories submenu appears.

4 If necessary, point to subfolder containing program to open it.

5 Click desired application name.

The program will run and a taskbar button with the application name will appear.

Open Applications with Associated Documents

An associated document is a file created in a particular application and identified by its file type extension. For example, a Microsoft Word document would be identified by the extension .doc. See Change File Types, page 175.

1 Open folder containing file you want to open.

2 Click desired document file icon to open it.

OR

1 Click **Start** .... 📕

2 Point to **Documents** .... 📄 Documents

3 Click desired document from list of documents.

The Documents menu contains recently opened documents.

Open Applications Using Run Command

1 Click **Start** .... 🔲

2 Click **Run**.. 🔲 Run..

The Run dialog box appears.

3 Type application path and filename............................*path\name*
   in **Open** text box.

   OR

   Click drop-down arrow to select commands
   previously entered in **Open** text box.

   OR

   Click Browse.. .... Alt + B
   to locate application to run. *See Use the*
   ***Browse Button**, page 146.*

4 Click OK .... Enter

APPLICATIONS

Exit from Windows Applications

Windows 98 will close Windows applications, but not MS-DOS applications, automatically when you shut down the computer.

- Click window **Close** button...☒

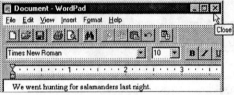

OR

1 Click **File** menu...**Alt**+**F**

2 Click E**x**it...**X**

OR

1 Right-click desired application taskbar button.

2 Click **Close**..**C**
  on shortcut menu that appears.

> 📖 *When you close an application, you may be prompted to save your work on a disk. See **Save Files from Windows Application**, page 169.*

> ✓ *To quickly close the selected application, press **Alt**+**F4**. If you press **Alt**+**F4** and no applications are running, however, you'll be prompted to shut down Windows.*

Terminate a Failed Application

Applications may fail to respond for a variety of reasons, such as program bugs (faults in the program code), interruptions in electrical power, or file corruption.

*Run **ScanDisk** after terminating a failed application. This procedure may fix file errors generated by the failed application and thus increase your system's stability. See your Windows 98 Help documentation for more information on ScanDisk.*

*Use the following procedure when an application freezes or fails to respond to the system. See **Restart Using Ctrl+Alt+Del**, page 3.*

1 Hold down **Ctrl** and **Alt** .... `Ctrl` + `Alt` + `Delete`
   while pressing **Delete** once.

   *The **Close Program** dialog box appears.*

2 Select program you want to close .... `↑` `↓`

3 Click `End Task` .... `Alt` + `E`

   Windows 98 will attempt to close the failed application.

4 Click `End Task` again, if prompted .... `Alt` + `E`

APPLICATIONS

MANAGE MULTIPLE APPLICATIONS

Windows 98 is designed to work with multiple applications at the same time, letting you arrange multiple windows for simultaneous viewing and allowing you to switch between applications with the click of the mouse.

Arrange Open Windows

You can arrange multiple application and folder windows on the screen so that you can view all, or some of them, at once.

1 Click **Minimize** button.. ⬚

in any window you do not want to arrange.

> 📖 *Windows that are minimized continue to run, but will not be arranged by the window command that follows.*

2 Right-click empty area on Windows 98 taskbar.

> 📖 *If you click a button, a **shortcut** menu will appear containing commands specific to the object you have clicked. To close the menu, press **Escape** or click a blank area off the menu.*

3 Click desired window command on shortcut menu:

- **Cascade Windows**.. 🅂

to display windows in overlapping sequence as shown below.

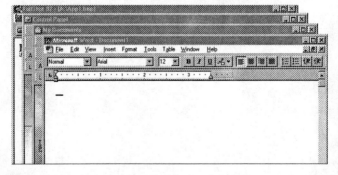

- **Tile Windows Horizontally** ....
  to display windows evenly from top to bottom
  as shown below.

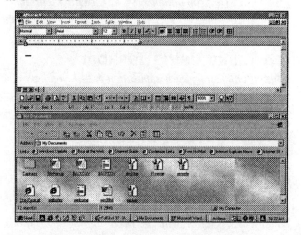

- **Tile Windows Vertically** ....
  to display windows evenly from left to right as shown below.

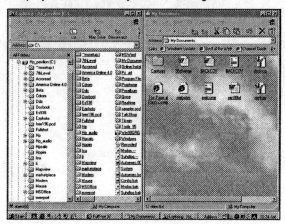

continued...

APPLICATIONS

Arrange Open Windows (cont.)

- **Minimize All Windows**..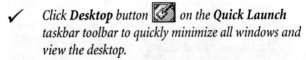

  to reduce all open windows to taskbar buttons.

  ✓ *Click **Desktop** button 🖥 on the **Quick Launch** taskbar toolbar to quickly minimize all windows and view the desktop.*

Switch Tasks Using Taskbar

Taskbar buttons appear for each application or task you have opened.

- Click desired application taskbar button to switch to that task.

  ✓ *If the taskbar gets crowded and the entire button name is not visible, rest your mouse pointer on a taskbar button to view its full name.*

Application window displays in front of other running windows.

Switch Tasks Using Keyboard

Using Windows 98, you can switch between running applications using the keyboard.

  ✓ *If you have assigned a shortcut key to an application, you can press it to quickly switch to that application. See **Keyboard Shortcuts**, page 42.*

1 Hold down **Alt** and press **Tab** until the desired task is highlighted.

*The **Task Switching** dialog box appears.*

2 Continue holding down **Alt** to keep the **Task Switching** dialog box in view.

  💣 *If you release **Alt**, the dialog box will disappear.*

3 Release keys to select highlighted item.

MS-DOS APPLICATIONS

*Using Windows 98, you can still run MS-DOS applications in a window or in full-screen mode. You can also run multiple MS-DOS applications at the same time. See DDC Publishing's **DOS 6.0-6.22 Quick Reference Guide** for more information on MS-DOS programs.*

Start MS-DOS Session and Run an Application

1 Click **Start** .... 🏢

2 Point to **Programs** .... 📁 Programs

3 Click **MS-DOS Prompt** .... 🖥 MS-DOS Prompt

An MS-DOS window appears.

To switch to folder containing application to run:

  a If necessary, change to drive containing application
     by typing drive letter followed by a colon ....*letter*:

  b Press **Enter** .... Enter

  c Use the CD command to change the folder containing
     the application (e.g., **CD\ "program files"**).

> 📖 *If you don't know the name of the folder that contains
> the program, change to the root directory and type the
> following:*
> **CD**
> **DIR *prgname* /s**
>
> *Substitute the actual name for **Prgname**.*

61

Applications

To switch between window and full-screen view:

- Hold down **Alt** and press **Enter** .... **Alt** + **Enter**
  to switch between window and full-screen view.

4 After using the application, exit program
with appropriate commands.

To exit MS-DOS window:

- Type *exit* on command line ....*exit*

  OR

  Click MS-DOS window **Close** button .... ☒

**SET MS-DOS APPLICATION SO COMMAND WINDOW
CLOSES WHEN APPLICATION CLOSES**

1 Run application in the window .... **Alt** + **Enter**

2 Right-click its title bar.

3 Click **Properties** .... ℝ

> *The application's **Properties** dialog box appears.*

4 Select **Close on exit** check box in **Program** tab.

5 Click [OK] .... Enter

WINDOWS 98

APPLICATIONS

Run MS-DOS Application Using Run Command

1 Click **Start** .... 🖼

2 Click **Run** .... 🔷 Run...

*The **Run** dialog box opens.*

3 Type application path and filename ....*path\name*
in **Open** text box.

*The path indicates the location of the application file on disk. It
starts with the letter of the drive followed by a colon (:) and a
backslash (\). The first-level folder name appears after that. If
additional folder names are required, separate the names with
backslashes. Finally, type a backslash and the application filename.*

OR

Click **Browse** to locate the application filename
in the hierarchy of folders on your computer. *See **Use
the Browse Button**, page 146.*

4 Click **OK** .... Enter

*If you use an application often, consider creating a shortcut to the
application and placing it on the desktop or on the **Start** menu. See
Create Shortcuts, page 96.*

APPLICATIONS

TRANSFER DATA AND OBJECTS BETWEEN APPLICATIONS

Windows 98 provides the clipboard and special commands (Cut, Copy, and Paste) so you can easily transfer data (or objects) from documents in one Windows application to another.

Cut, Copy, and Paste Data Using Clipboard

*When you cut or copy data, Windows stores that data in the **clipboard**, a temporary storage area. You can paste data stored in the clipboard to another location in the same document, or into a document created in a different application as needed. Data placed on the clipboard will remain there only until you cut or copy again, or until you exit Windows.*

> *When transferring data, the source and destination applications must support the data type you're transferring. For example, if you are transferring graphic data into a word processing document, the word processor application must be able to accept graphic data.*

1 Open source and destination documents.

2 Select source document.

   Click the application on the taskbar to select it.

3 Select the data you wish to copy or move.

   To copy data to the clipboard:

   a Click **Edit** menu .... `Alt` + `E`

   b Click **Copy** .... `C`

   OR

   Press **Ctrl** while pressing **C** .... `Ctrl` + `C`

To cut (move) data to the clipboard:

a Click **Edit** menu .... `Alt` + `E`

b Click **Cut** .... `T`

OR

Press **Ctrl** while pressing **X** .... `Ctrl` + `X`

4 Select document to receive data, if necessary.

5 Place insertion point where you want to insert new data.

a Click **Edit** menu .... `Alt` + `E`

b Click **Paste** .... `P`

OR

Press **Ctrl** while pressing **V** .... `Ctrl` + `V`

Windows copies the data into the document at the insertion point.

6 Click outside highlighted data object to return to
normal editing mode.

Display Clipboard Viewer

1 Click **Start** .... 🔲

2 Point to **Programs** .... 🔲 Programs

3 Point to **Accessories** .... 🔲 Accessories

4 Point to **System Tools** .... 🔲 System Tools

5 Click **Clipboard Viewer** .... 🔲 Clipboard Viewer

*The **Clipboard Viewer** window displays the clipboard's current
contents.*

APPLICATIONS

INSERTING OLE OBJECTS IN DOCUMENTS

*Windows supports **Object Linking and Embedding (OLE)**. This lets you insert embedded or linked objects into a document. An object is a collection of information created with an OLE object application, such as Paint. A container application is one that can receive OLE objects, such as WordPad.*

> ***Embedded objects:*** *When you insert an embedded object, Windows inserts the object as a copy in the document. You can edit the embedded object in-place from within the document. This means the object application menus and tools replace the container application menu and tools while you edit the object.*

> ***Linked objects:*** *When you insert a linked object, Windows inserts a connection to the object in the document. You can edit a linked object from any document that has received the object. When you edit a linked object, all other documents with links to that object are updated automatically.*

Insert an OLE Object

> *The destination application file must support object linking and embedding. Most software designed to run with Windows supports OLE; consult your software documentation if you're not sure.*

1 Place insertion point in destination file where you want to insert object.

2 Click **Insert** menu .... `Alt` + `I`

3 Click **Object** .... `O`

*The **Insert Object** dialog box appears. This dialog box and its commands will vary slightly from application to application.*

INSERT EXISTING OBJECT

1 Complete steps 1-3, **Insert OLE Object**, page 66.

2 Select **Create from File** option button .... `Alt`+`F`

   The Insert Object dialog box appears.

3 Type path and filename .... *path\name*
   of object to insert in **File** text box.

   OR

   Click `Browse...` .... `Alt`+`B`
   to locate and select the file to insert. *See Use
   the Browse Button, page 146.*

4 Select **Link** check box if you want changes to source
   document to automatically affect inserted object.

5 Click `OK` .... `Enter`

   *The object is inserted, and menus and tools for the application it
   belongs to appear in the destination application. Edit the object as
   desired. Then click outside the object to hide its application tools
   and return to normal editing mode.*

CREATE AND INSERT NEW OLE OBJECT

1 Complete steps 1-3, **Insert OLE Object**, page 66.

2 Select **Create New** option button .... `Alt`+`N`

3 Select object type to create from **Object Type** list.

4 Click `OK` .... `Enter`

   *The menus and tools for the application where you can create the
   new object appear in the destination application window.*

5 Use appropriate application tools to create desired object.

6 Click outside object to return to normal editing mode.

APPLICATIONS

Work With OLE Objects

To select inserted OLE object:

- Click object.

Handles appear on the object.

sizing handles

With the object selected, you can:

- *Press* **Delete** *key to delete object.*
- *Point to object, click, and drag to move object.*
- *Drag sizing handles to change size and shape of object.*

To activate inserted OLE object:

- Double-click object.

The source application tools replace the destination application tools.

With the object activated, you can work with its source application tools to change the object.

USE CHANNELS

*You can view Web content that is "pushed" to your computer in a stream that resembles the television experience. Channel data can be delivered in ways that surpass static Web pages, providing wider views and faster access to enriched Web content. You can subscribe to channels to view them offline. When you subscribe to a **channel**, its content appears on the desktop as an **Active Desktop item**, and the provider updates it on a regular basis. See **Create Active Desktop Item from Gallery**, page 76.*

Display Channel Bar on Desktop

*Use the **Channel bar** to quickly open Web sites from the desktop without first opening the browser.*

1 Click **Start** ....

2 Point to **Settings** .... **Settings**

3 Point to **Active Desktop** .... **Active Desktop**

4 Click **Customize my Desktop** .... **C**

5 Select **View my Active Desktop** .... **V**
as a web page check box.

*The list box on the **Web** tab lists all the Active Desktop items that you have downloaded. The preview area shows the position of each Active Desktop item you have displayed.*

6 Select **Internet Explorer Channel Bar** check box.

7 Click **OK** .... **Enter**

THE DESKTOP

Remove Channel Bar from Desktop

1 Move mouse pointer over top of **Channel bar**.

2 Click **Close** button... ⊠
when it appears.

Close

Open Channel Bar

📖 *To view channels, you must have an Internet connection.*

✧ From the Taskbar

- Click **View Channels** button ....
on **Quick Launch** toolbar.

*Windows 98 will launch **Internet Explorer**.*

✧ From Internet Explorer

- Click **View Channels** button..
on **Internet Explorer Standard** toolbar.

*The **Channel bar** appears in the left pane. The current Web page remains in the right pane until you select a channel.*

✧ From Any Folder Window

1 Click **View** menu.. Alt + V

2 Point to **Explorer Bar** .... E

3 Click **Channels** C

*Internet Explorer opens. The **Channel bar** appears in the left pane, and the **Active Channel Guide** appears in the right pane.*

View Channels

☞ From the Internet Explorer

- Click channel in left pane to view its contents in right pane.

☞ From the Desktop

- Click desired channel on **Channel bar**.

  OR

  a Right-click the channel you want to view on
  the **Channel bar**.

  b Click **Open Channel** on the shortcut menu that appears.

You do not have to subscribe to a channel to view it.

*The **Channel bar** appears in the left pane, and the **Active Channel Guide** appears in the right pane. See **Display Channel Bar on Desktop**, page 69.*

✓ *Rest the mouse pointer on a channel to read a description of it.*

Add/Remove Channels on Channel Bar

*You can use the channels that appear on the **Channel bar** right away, or you can use the **Active Channel Guide** to add channels available through the Microsoft Web site. When you add a channel, you can subscribe to it so that the content is delivered to you at regular intervals.*

THE DESKTOP

Add Channel to Channel Bar

1 Open the **Channel bar**. *See Open Channel Bar, page 70.*

2 Click 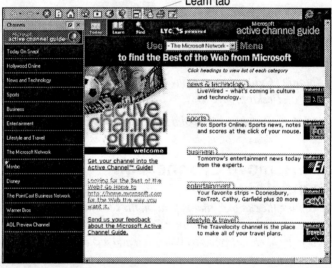 at the top of **Channel bar**.

Windows 98 will connect to the Internet and the Active Channel Guide will open. The Channel bar will appear in the left frame and the Active Channel Guide will appear in the right frame.

    Click the Learn tab for help on how to use the Active Channel Guide.

3 Click the heading tab you want to view.

The Find page appears with a list of channels for the selected category.

4 Choose range of channels to view in left-hand **Findings** bar.

Channel logos or names appear.

    You can also enter topic names for the channels you want to look for and click the Find button.

Add Channel to Channel Bar (cont.)

5 Click logo or name of channel you want to preview.

Depending on the content and your connection speed, it may take some time for the entire preview and the Add Active Channel button to appear.

6 Click **Add Active Channel** button ....

The Add Active Channel(TM) content dialog box appears.

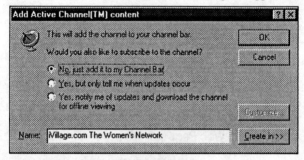

7 Select desired subscription options.

8 Click .... Enter

Remove Channel from Channel Bar

1 Right-click channel you want to remove.

2 Click **Delete** .... D

on shortcut menu that appears.

3 Click .... Enter

to send channel to **Recycle Bin**.

See The Recycle Bin, page 25.

THE DESKTOP

THE ACTIVE DESKTOP

You can place active content (news, stock tickers, weather) from Web pages or channels you subscribe to on the desktop. Most Active Desktop features require access to the Internet. You can add (subscribe to) standard Web pages to the desktop.

Enable the Active Desktop

1 Right-click desktop.

   OR

   a Click **Start** ....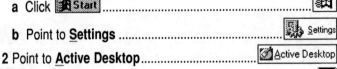

   b Point to **Settings** ....

2 Point to **Active Desktop** ....

3 Select **View as Web Page** ....

View or Change Active Desktop Options

1 Right-click desktop.

   OR

   a Click **Start** ....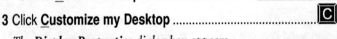

   b Point to **Settings** ....

2 Point to **Active Desktop** ....

3 Click **Customize my Desktop** ....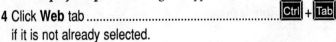

   *The **Display Properties** dialog box appears.*

4 Click **Web** tab .... Ctrl + Tab

   if it is not already selected.

*The following table describes options available on the **Web** tab of the **Display Properties** dialog box:*

<u>V</u>iew my Active Desktop as a web page check box	Enables Active Desktop features.
List of Active Desktop Items	Lists available Active Desktop items you have already downloaded. To show an item on the desktop, click to select check box beside it.
New	Creates new Active Desktop items.
<u>D</u>elete	Erases selected item.
Properties	Changes subscription settings for selected item.
Reset All	Removes all created items from desktop, except Internet Explorer Channel Bar.

CHANGE SUBSCRIPTION PROPERTIES
FOR ACTIVE DESKTOP ITEMS

1 Select subscription you want to change.

2 Click Properties .... Alt + R

3 Select desired tab and set desired options:

- **Subscription** tab .... Ctrl + Tab

  displays a summary of the subscription and lets you unsubscribe to it.

- **Receiving** tab .... Ctrl + Tab

  lets you set notification options; the Advanced command lets you specify what content to download.

- **Schedule** tab .... Ctrl + Tab

  lets you specify how and when to update (download) Web content.

THE DESKTOP

Create Active Desktop Item from Gallery

You can preview and install Active Desktop items (stock ticker, weather, etc.) from the Microsoft Active Desktop Gallery. You must have an Internet connection to access the Microsoft Web site.

1 Right-click desktop.

2 Click **Properties** .... R
   on shortcut menu that appears.

   The Display Properties dialog box appears.

3 Click **Web** tab .... Ctrl + Tab

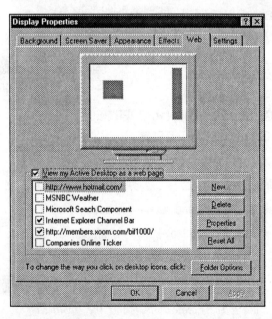

4 Select **View my Active Desktop as a Web page**..... Alt + V
   if necessary.

5 Click .... N

Create Active Desktop Item (cont.)

The New Active Desktop Item dialog box appears.

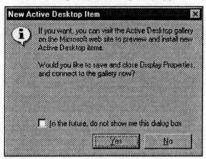

6 Click [Yes] .... Y

to select channel from Microsoft Active Desktop
Gallery Web site.

7 Select item to add to your Active Desktop following
the instructions on the Active Desktop Gallery Web site.

8 Click **Add to Active Desktop** .... Add to Active Desktop

9 Click [Yes] .... Y

to add the item to your Active Desktop.

*The Add item to Active Desktop dialog box then appears,
showing the name and address of the Web site.*

10 Click [OK] .... Enter

Windows will download the subscription for the channel.

11 Close the Active Desktop Gallery Web Site.

The Active Desktop item will appear on your desktop.

THE DESKTOP

Add Web Sites as Active Desktop Items

1 Right-click desktop.

2 Click **Properties** .... R

   The Display Properties dialog box appears.

3 Click **Web** tab .... Ctrl + Tab

4 Select **View my Active Desktop as a Web page** ..... Alt + V
   if necessary.

5 Click New... .... N

   The New Active Desktop Item dialog box appears.

6 Click No .... N

   to add any Web site other than those in the Microsoft
   Active Desktop Gallery Web site to your desktop.

   *The New Active Desktop Item dialog box appears, where you can
   browse for a Web site to add to your desktop.*

7 Type Web site address .... *address*
   OR
   Click Browse... .... Alt + B
   to locate file. *See Use the Browse Button, page 146.*

8 Click OK .... Enter

   Windows 98 will connect to the Internet.

   *The Add item to Active Desktop dialog box then appears,
   showing the name and address of the Web site.*

9 Click OK .... Enter

   Windows 98 will download the subscription for the Web site.

10 Click OK to close **Display Properties** dialog box.

   *From Internet Explorer, you can also right-click any
   link on a Web page, drag it to the desktop, and then
   select Create Active Desktop item(s) Here.*

THE DESKTOP

CHANGE DESKTOP PROPERTIES

Windows 98 makes it easy to change the appearance of screen elements, such as the background, screen saver, icon appearance, and desktop theme settings.

Open Display Properties Dialog Box

⌧ From the Desktop

1 Right-click desktop.

2 Click **Properties** .... 🇷

⌧ From Control Panel

1 Click **Start** .... 🏭

2 Point to **Settings** .... 🔧 Settings

3 Point to **Control Panel** .... 🖥 Control Panel

4 Click **Display** icon .... 🖥 Display

THE DESKTOP

Change Desktop Appearance

You can set colors and fonts for windows and menus.

1 Open **Display Properties** dialog box. *See Open the Display Properties Dialog Box, page 79.*

2 Click **Appearance** tab .... Ctrl + Tab

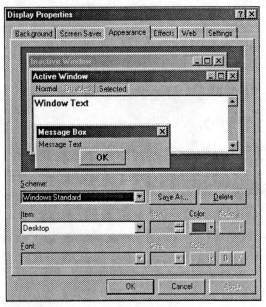

*The **sample area** shows the current appearance of screen elements.*

     *You can click the **Apply** button to see how the new settings will look without closing the dialog box.*

To select a predefined scheme:

Choose from color schemes that Windows 98 has defined, including Brick, Desert, Eggplant, Rose, and Storm.

a Click **Scheme** drop-down list arrow .... S

b Select desired scheme from list that appears .... ↑ ↓

To change a screen item:

Change the color scheme and font type of screen items, including the active title bar, application background, caption buttons, icons, and menus.

a Click desired screen element in **sample area**.

The screen element name appears in the item box automatically.

   OR

   i Click **Item** drop-down list arrow I

   ii Click item you want to change.

b Set desired options for item.

Available settings, which may include Size, Color, Font, and Font Color, will depend on the selected item.

To save the current settings as a scheme:

a Click Save As V

b Type desired name of scheme ....*name*
   in text box provided.

c Click OK .... Enter

3 Click OK .... Enter
to close **Display Properties** dialog box.

THE DESKTOP

Change Desktop Background

Choose a wallpaper or pattern for the desktop. The wallpaper can be an HTML document or a picture file. See **Select a Web page as Desktop Wallpaper**, *page 83.*

1 Open **Display Properties** dialog box. *See* **Open Display Properties Dialog Box**, *page 79.*

2 Click **Background** tab...

The **sample area** *shows a preview of the selected background, wallpaper, and pattern.*

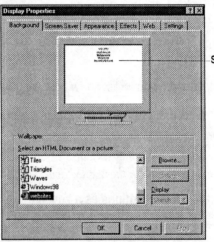

sample area

3 Click background you want to use in **Select an HTML Document or a picture** list box.

OR

Click .... **Alt** + **B**

to locate a graphic or HTML file stored on your computer. *See* **Use the Browse Button**, *page 146.*

📖 *You can use most graphic files, such as bitmaps (.bmp), GIFs (.gif), and JPEG (.jpeg) images, as wallpaper.*

4 Click **Display** drop-down list .... `Alt` + `D`

and select the display of the wallpaper picture:

- **Center**   Centers wallpaper image.
- **Tile**   Covers your entire screen
with a small wallpaper image.
- **Stretch**   Stretches wallpaper image
to fill screen area.

📖 *You can use patterns and wallpaper simultaneously.
However, if **Tile** is selected, you cannot see the pattern.*

5 Click Apply to preview changes .... `Alt` + `A`

before you close dialog box.

OR

Click OK to accept changes .... `Enter`

and close dialog box.

SELECT A WEB PAGE AS DESKTOP WALLPAPER

📖 *You can also right-click any graphic on a Web page,
then click **Set as Wallpaper** on the shortcut menu that
appears.*

1 Open **Display Properties** dialog box. *See **Open
Display Properties Dialog Box**, page 79.*

2 Click **Background** tab .... `Ctrl` + `Tab`

3 Click Browse .... `Alt` + `B`

to locate and select an HTML document stored on
your computer. *See **Use the Browse Button**, page 146.*

4 Click OK to accept changes .... `Enter`

and close dialog box.

THE DESKTOP

SELECT BACKGROUND PATTERN FOR DESKTOP

1 Open **Display Properties** dialog box. *See Open Display Properties Dialog Box, page 79.*

2 Click **Background** tab.. Ctrl + Tab

3 Select **None** from **Wallpaper** list box.

4 Click Pattern... .... Alt + P

   to choose patterned background.

   The Pattern dialog box opens.

5 Select desired pattern.

6 Click OK .... Enter

   to close **Pattern** dialog box.

7 Click OK to accept changes and close **Display Properties** dialog box.

Change Desktop Effects

Windows 98 has grouped miscellaneous desktop and screen effects on the Display Properties Effects tab. It includes options to change icons for system folders, hide icons when the desktop is viewed as a Web page, and a variety of visual effects such as the setting to show window content while dragging.

CHANGE APPEARANCE OF DESKTOP ICONS

1 Open **Display Properties** dialog box. *See Open Display Properties Dialog Box, page 79.*

2 Click **Effects** tab... Ctrl + Tab

3 Click icon you want to change in **Desktop icons** scroll box.

4 Click Change Icon... .... Alt + C

THE DESKTOP

Change Appearance of Icons (cont.)

To use an icon from the default icon file:

▪ Double-click icon in the **Current icon** list.

To use an icon from another icon file:

▪ Click .... Alt + B
to locate and select desired icon file. *See Use
the Browse Button, page 146.*

5 Click [OK   ] .... Enter

CHANGE WEB PAGE AND VISUAL EFFECTS

1 Open **Display Properties** dialog box. *See Open
Display Properties Dialog Box, page 79.*

2 Click **Effects** tab .... Ctrl + Tab

3 Select/deselect desired setting in **Visual Effects** area.

> *Consider deselecting **Use large icons** and **Show icons**
> **using all possible colors** to increase available memory
> and performance on your system. If **Show window**
> **contents while dragging** is selected, you will not be
> able to see through the window as you drag it.*

THE DESKTOP

Change Desktop Screen Saver

*The Windows 98 **screen saver** feature will start when your computer is idle for a specified number of minutes. If you protect the screen saver with a password, you can ensure that others cannot use your system when you are away from it. You can also select a Channel screen saver if you have subscribed to a channel that provides this feature.*

1 Open **Display Properties** dialog box. *See **Open Display Properties Dialog Box**, page 79.*

2 Click **Screen Saver** tab... `Ctrl` + `Tab`

3 Select screen saver you want to use in **Screen Saver** list box.

The sample area shows a preview of the selected screen saver.

> 📖 *Select **None** at the top of the list to turn the screen saver off.*

4 Click `Preview` .... `Alt` + `V`

to preview selected screen saver from list on your desktop.

5 Click `Settings...` .... `Alt` + `T`

to customize screen saver.

*Options will depend on the screen saver you select. If you select **Channel Screen Saver**, you must click the **Settings** button to select a channel.*

*To use **Channel data** as a screen saver, you must first subscribe to a channel that supports the screen saver feature. Once you do this, the name of the channel(s) will appear when you click the **Settings** button after selecting **Channel Screen Saver** in the **Screen Saver** list box.*

6 Select or type the number of minutes your computer is idle before Windows 98 starts the screen saver in **Wait** increment box.

Change Screen Saver (cont.)

To password-protect the screen saver:

a Select **P**assword protect check box.....................`Alt`+`P`

b Click `Change...`..`Alt`+`C`

*The **Change Password** dialog box opens.*

c Type password...*password*
   and confirmation password when prompted.

d Click `OK`..`Enter`

*The **Change Password** dialog box closes.*

> 💣 *If you forget your password, you will not be able to gain access to your system without restarting it.*

7 Click `OK` to accept changes.....................................`Enter`
   and close dialog box.

> 📖 *You can move your mouse or press any key to clear the screen saver after it has started. If you assigned a password to the screen saver, you will be prompted to supply it.*

THE DESKTOP

Change Desktop Themes

*Windows 98 comes with **desktop themes** that coordinate your display settings, including icons and sounds, into a predesigned theme. You can customize an existing theme by changing different desktop elements. You can also create a new theme by saving your changes to an existing theme under a new name.*

✓ *Save your current desktop settings as a theme so you can return to them if you desire.*

1 Click **Start** ....

2 Point to **Settings** .... Settings

3 Click **Control Panel** .... Control Panel

📖 *If **Desktop Themes** is missing from **Control Panel**, see **Add or Remove Windows Components**, page 50, for information on installing this feature.*

4 Click **Desktop Themes** icon .... Desktop Themes

*The **Desktop Themes** dialog box appears.*

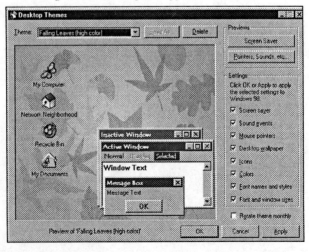

Change Desktop Themes (cont.)

5 Select desired theme from **Theme** list box.

6 Click `Screen Saver` .... `Alt` + `R`

to preview the selected theme's screen saver.

7 Press **Escape** .... `Esc`

to exit preview.

8 Click `Pointers, Sounds, etc...` .... `Alt` + `P`

to preview theme's mouse pointers and sound effects.

> *If you don't want to use one of the theme's desktop
> items, make sure its check box is blank in the **Settings**
> area of the **Desktop Themes** dialog box.*

9 Click `Close` to exit preview.

10 Click `OK` to accept changes .... `Enter`

and close dialog box.

THE DESKTOP

Change Display Settings

You can change or view a variety of display settings, such as the monitor and adapter type, color settings, and screen area (resolution), from the Settings tab in the Display Properties dialog box.

1 Open **Display Properties** dialog box. *See Open Display Properties Dialog Box, page 79.*

2 Click **Settings** tab..

*The **Display** area shows the current monitor and display adapter, which determines the range of options you can select. For example, the monitor type may limit the **Screen area** range to 800 by 600 pixels.*

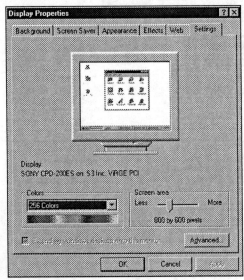

To change monitor color settings:

▪ Select number of colors that you want your monitor to display from **Colors** drop-down list.

To change screen area:

▪ Drag **Screen area** slider bar to change screen resolution.

To set advanced display options:

a Click `Advanced...` ....`Alt`+`D`

*The **Advanced** dialog box opens.*

b Set desired options for your monitor and display adapter.
Consult your hardware manuals for further information.

c Click `OK` to accept changes ....`Enter`
and close the **Advanced** dialog box.

3 Click `OK` ....`Enter`
to close **Display Properties** dialog box.

*When you click `OK` or `Apply` in the **Display**
Properties dialog box, another dialog box will appear telling
you that Windows 98 will resize your desktop.*

Arrange (Sort) Icons
*You can sort file and folder icons on the desktop, in a folder window, in
the Windows Explorer **Contents** pane, in the Find results list, or in
common dialog boxes. Sort options depend on the type of folder or
workspace the icons are stored in.*

1 Right-click empty area of folder or workspace.

OR

Click **View** menu ....`Alt`+`V`
in folder window.

continued...

THE DESKTOP

Arrange Icons (cont.)

2 Point to **Arrange Icons** I

3 Click desired sort option, which may include the following:

- by **Name** .... N
- by **Type** .... T
- by **Size** .... Z
- by **Date** .... D
- **Auto Arrange** .... A

The Auto Arrange option arranges icons so that they fit tightly within the folder space and reorder themselves when the window size changes. This option is available when the view of folder icons is set to Large Icons or Small Icons. See Change View of Folder Icons, below.

To quickly line up icons on the desktop:

a Right-click desktop.

b Click **Line Up Icons** .... U
on shortcut menu that appears.

Change View of Folder Icons

1 Click **View** menu .... Alt + V
in folder window.

OR

a Right-click empty area of folder or workspace.

b Point to **View** V
on shortcut menu that appears.

2 Select desired sort option:

- **Large Icons** .... [G]

  when there are a small number of icons, and you want the option to arrange the icons by dragging them.

- **Small Icons** .... [M]

  to view more icons in a given window, and you want to be able to arrange the icons by dragging them.

- **List** .... [L]

  when you want to view icons in a compact list, and you will not need to drag icons to arrange them.

- **Details** .... [D]

  when you want to view information about the file, such as file size and last modification date, and when you want to sort the icons by clicking the column headings.

THE DESKTOP

Change Time and Date

Windows 98 displays the current time in the notification area of the taskbar.

1 Double-click taskbar clock .... `11:58 AM`

OR

a Click **Start** ....

b Point to **Settings** .... `Settings`

c Click **Control Panel** .... `Control Panel`

d Click **Date/Time** icon .... Date/Time

*The **Date/Time Properties** dialog box appears.*

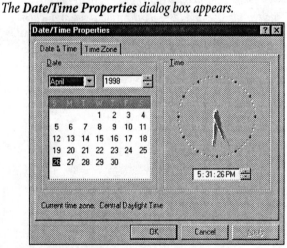

To view the current date setting:

▪ Rest mouse pointer on time displayed in notification area of taskbar.

WINDOWS 98
THE DESKTOP

Change Time/Date (cont.)

To change the date or time:

a Click **Date & Time** tab .... `Ctrl` + `Tab`
if necessary.

b Select desired date using the month drop-down
list box and year boxes as well as the calendar
list scroll box.

c Type time in time text box .... *time*

To change time zone:

a Click **Time Zone** tab .... `Ctrl` + `Tab`

b Select time zone from drop-down list box provided.

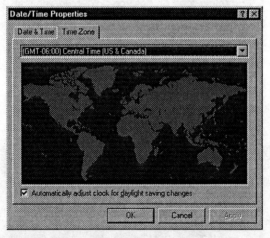

To adjust clock for daylight saving time:

- Select/deselect **Automatically adjust clock for** .... `Alt` + `D`
daylight saving changes check box.

2 Click  OK .... `Enter`

95

THE DESKTOP

Create Shortcuts

Shortcuts are links to items you use often, such as applications, network computers, documents, folders, printers, and shared items on other computers. Instead of browsing folders or menus each time you want to open an item, you can create a shortcut to that item and place it on the desktop or in a folder. Shortcut icons always have a jump arrow in the lower-left corner.

CREATE SHORTCUTS FROM DESTINATION FOLDER

Use this procedure when you want to create shortcuts in the current folder to items in other folders.

1 Right-click empty area on desktop, folder workspace, Windows Explorer **Contents** pane, or common dialog box workspace.

2 Point to **New** .... ⊞

on shortcut menu that appears.

3 Click **Shortcut** .... ▣ Shortcut

*The **Create Shortcut** dialog box appears.*

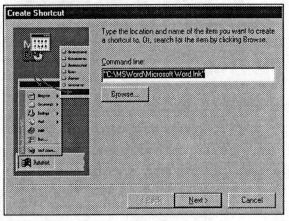

Create Shortcuts from Destination Folder (cont.)

4 Type path and filename of item ....*path\name*

you want to create shortcut to in **Command line**.

OR

Click 🟦Browse🟦 ....**Alt** + **R**

to browse your computer system for the file. *See*
Use the Browse Button, *page 146.*

5 Click 🟦Next >🟦 ....**Alt** + **N**

6 Type or edit shortcut name..*name*

in text box provided.

7 Click 🟦Finish🟦 ....**Enter**

CREATE SHORTCUTS FROM SOURCE FOLDER

*Use any of the three procedures below when you are in a folder
containing an item for which you want to create a shortcut. Also, use
these procedures when you want to place the shortcut on the desktop
or in another folder.*

CREATE SHORTCUTS BY RIGHT-CLICKING

📖 *This procedure applies only to files and folders.*

1 Right-click item you want to create shortcut to.

2 Click **Copy** ....**C**

on shortcut menu that appears.

3 Open destination folder.

The destination folder can be a folder window or the desktop.

4 Right-click empty area in desktop or folder workspace.

5 Click **Paste Shortcut**...**S**

on shortcut menu that appears.

THE DESKTOP

CREATE SHORTCUTS BY RIGHT-DRAGGING

1 Arrange desktop so the item you want to create a shortcut to and the destination folder are in view.

The destination folder can be an icon, the desktop, or a folder window.

2 Right-drag item you want to create a shortcut to onto destination folder.

3 Click **Create Shortcut(s) Here** on menu that appears.

CREATE SHORTCUTS USING MENU

1 Arrange desktop so the item to you want to create a shortcut to and the destination folder are in view.

The destination folder can be an icon, the desktop, or a folder window.

2 Select item you want to create a shortcut to.

3 Click **File** menu...**Alt** + **F**

4 Click **Create Shortcut** ....**S**

Windows 98 creates the shortcut in the source folder.

5 Drag shortcut icon onto destination folder.

Destination folder can be an icon, the desktop, or a folder window.

CHANGE SHORTCUT PROPERTIES

*From a shortcut's **Properties** dialog box, you can specify the folder to use when first opening or saving files, assign a keyboard shortcut to open the shortcut, and specify how to display the item when it is opened.*

1 Right-click desired shortcut icon.

2 Click **Properties** .... Ⓡ

on shortcut menu that appears.

*The shortcut's **Properties** dialog box appears.*

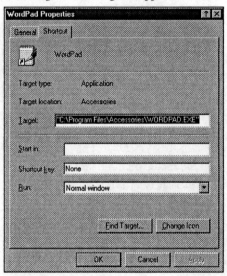

3 Click **Shortcut** tab .... Ctrl + Tab

To change name and location of item shortcut points to:

- Type path and filename .... *path\name*
  in **Target** text box.

📖 *It isn't necessary to put quotes around the path you type.*

continued...

THE DESKTOP

Shortcut Properties (cont.)

To specify folder to use when first opening shortcut item:

- Type path to folder...*path*
  in **Start in** text box.

    📖 *The path typed here specifies the location of files the application uses, such as the folder to use when first opening or saving files.*

To assign a keyboard shortcut:

a Click in **Shortcut key** text box.

b Press the keys you want to use as a shortcut.

    📖 *If the shortcut key you assign conflicts with a command in a Windows application, the application's command will no longer work.*

To specify how to display item when it is opened:

- Select desired option in **Run** drop-down list box.

    📖 *You can choose from **Normal window**, **Maximized**, or **Minimized**.*

4 Click [OK] ....Enter

CHANGE TASKBAR AND START MENU APPEARANCE

*You can customize taskbar and **Start** menu properties to match your working style. For example, you can reduce the size and space between items on the **Start** menu, or hide the taskbar when it is not in use. You can also add and remove items from the **Start** menu, as well as rearrange their order.*

Change Taskbar and Start Menu Properties

1 a Right-click empty area on taskbar.

  b Click **Properties** .... Ⓡ
  on shortcut menu that appears.

  OR

  a Click 🏁 **Start** .... 🪟

  b Point to **Settings** .... 🗔 Settings

  c Click **Taskbar & Start Menu** .... 🗗 Taskbar & Start Menu...

*The **Taskbar Properties** dialog box appears.*

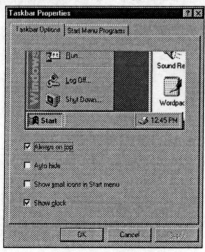

continued...

THE DESKTOP

Taskbar/Start Menu Properties (cont.)

2 Select/deselect the desired options:

- **Always on top**.. `Alt`+`T`

  to ensure the taskbar is always visible.

- **Auto hide** .... `Alt`+`U`

  *to reduce the taskbar to a thin line when
  it is not in use. To view the taskbar, rest the mouse
  pointer on it.*

- **Show small icons in Start menu** .... `Alt`+`S`

  *to reduce the size of and space between items on
  the Start menu. Then you can move your favorite
  shortcuts in the Programs folder to the top of the
  Start menu to reduce the number of mouse actions
  it takes to open them.*

- **Show clock** .... `Alt`+`C`

  to show the clock in the notification area.

✓ *Click the **Help** button (the pointer becomes a ▷?)
  then click the setting you want help with. A pop-up
  window appears with a description of the setting.*

3 Click [OK] to accept changes .... `Enter`
  and close dialog box.

Add Items to Start Menu

*You can add a menu item (shortcut) to the top of the **Start** menu, the **Programs** menu, or to a Programs submenu.*

1 Click ![Start] .... 🏛

2 Point to **Settings**... 🏛 Settings

3 Click **Taskbar & Start Menu** .... 🏛 Taskbar & Start Menu...

*The **Taskbar Properties** dialog box appears.*

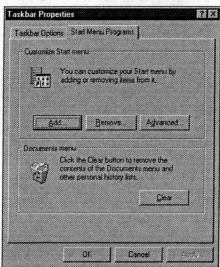

4 Click **Start Menu Programs** tab .... Ctrl + Tab

5 Click ![Add...] .... Alt + A

*The **Create Shortcut** dialog box appears.*

6 Type path and filename ....*path\name*
for menu item in **Command line**.

OR

Click ![Browse...] .... Alt + R

to locate file. *See **Use the Browse Button**, page 146.*

continued...

THE DESKTOP

Add Items to Start Menu (cont.)

7 Click [Next >] .... Alt + N

The Select Program Folder dialog box appears.

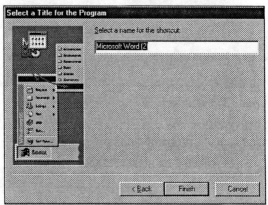

8 Select folder in which to place shortcut.

> 📖 *You can click New Folder... to create a new folder in the Start menu folder.*

9 Click [Next >] .... Alt + N

The Select a Title for the Program dialog box appears.

THE DESKTOP

Add Items to Start Menu (cont.)

10 Type shortcut name...*name*

You can use the name Windows 98 suggests.

11 Click [Finish] ....[Enter]

ADD ITEM TO START MENU BY DRAGGING

1 Find or open folder containing item to add to top of **Start** menu.

2 Drag item icon onto [Start] and continue to hold mouse button until Windows opens the **Start** menu.

3 While holding mouse button, move pointer to desired location on **Start** menu.

Windows indicates the insertion point with a horizontal bar.

4 Point to subfolders, if desired, to open them.

5 Release mouse button to add item to **Start** menu.

Clear Items on Documents Menu

*You can clear all shortcuts to recently opened documents on the **Documents** menu.*

1 Click [Start] ....[📖]

2 Point to **Settings**.....................................[🖳 Settings]

3 Click **Taskbar & Start Menu**..................[🖳 Taskbar & Start Menu...]

*The **Taskbar Properties** dialog box appears.*

4 Click **Start Menu Programs** tab ....[Ctrl]+[Tab]

5 Click [Clear] ....[Alt]+[C]
in **Documents menu** section.

6 Click [OK]

THE DESKTOP

Remove Items from Start Menu

*You can remove **Start** menu items (folders and shortcuts) from the top of the **Start** menu or one of its subfolders, such as the **Programs** folder.*

REMOVE START MENU ITEMS USING MENU

1 Click **Start** .... 📖

2 Point to **Settings** .... 🗂 Settings

3 Click **Taskbar & Start Menu** .... 🗔 Taskbar & Start Menu...

*The **Taskbar Properties** dialog box appears.*

4 Click **Start Menu Programs** tab .... Ctrl + Tab

5 Click **Remove** .... Alt + R

*The **Remove Shortcuts/Folders** dialog box appears.*

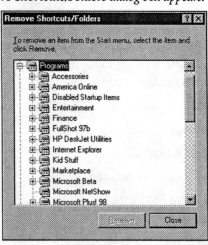

For steps 6 and 7, you may have to use the scroll arrows to bring the desired folder or shortcut into view.

6 Double-click folder icon containing item to remove, if necessary.

7 Click file or folder icon to remove.

> 📖 *If you select a folder, you will remove all the shortcuts
> and other folders it may contain.*

8 Click 【Remove.】 .... 🇷

9 Repeat steps 6–8 for each item to remove.

DELETE START MENU ITEM QUICKLY

1 Open **Start** menu and subfolder containing item to delete.

2 Right-click the item.

3 Click **Delete** .... 🇩
on shortcut menu that appears.

4 Click 【 OK 】 .... Enter

Arrange Items on Start Menu

*Windows 98 lets you move **Start** menu items directly from the menu
and to other menu positions (including **Start** menu subfolders) using
drag and drop. Additionally, you can drag and drop to move or copy
Start menu items to the desktop or other folders.*

1 Click 【 Start 】 .... 🪟

2 Point to any menu item with a triangle ▶
which means that a submenu is available.

3 Drag desired item to new location on **Start** menu.

*You can drag the item to any subfolder. As you move the item, the
insertion bar moves and subfolders open or close depending on the
position of your mouse.*

You can drag items off the menu to the desktop or another folder.

> 📖 *Press* Ctrl *while dragging the item to copy the item.
> When you are copying an item on the menu, a plus
> sign appears on the mouse pointer.*

THE DESKTOP

Customize Taskbar Toolbars

*Windows 98 lets you add predefined toolbars, such as the **Links**
toolbar or **Address bar**, to the taskbar. You can also create your
own toolbars. You can also move toolbars to floating positions, away
from the taskbar.*

Add or Remove Taskbar Toolbars

1 Right-click empty area of taskbar.

2 Point to **Toolbars** .... **T**
on shortcut menu that appears.

3 Select/deselect the desired toolbar:

- **Address** .... **A**
  *to open a local computer or Internet address
  by selecting its name. See **Use Address Bar to Access
  a Site**, page 183.*

- **Links** .... **L**
  *lets you access frequently used Internet links.
  See **Use Links Toolbar to Access the Web**, page 181.*

- **Desktop** .... **D**
  lets you access items on your desktop from the toolbar.

- **Quick Launch** .... **Q**
  lets you start programs with one mouse click.

Add Shortcut to Quick Launch Toolbar

- Drag and drop a shortcut or program file onto the
  Quick Launch toolbar.

  ✓ *Windows 98 creates a shortcut in the form of a button.
  A vertical bar indicates the insertion point.*

THE DESKTOP

Create New Toolbar

*You can select any folder as a new toolbar, including system folders such as **My Computer**. The toolbar will then display the items the folder contains.*

> ✓ *Customize your own toolbar by creating a folder on your hard disk and placing the shortcuts you want on your toolbar in the new folder. Then make the folder into a toolbar. See **Create Folder**, page 164 and **Move or Copy Folders and Files**, page 157.*

1 Right-click empty area on taskbar.

2 Point to **T**oolbars .... T

3 Click **N**ew Toolbar .... N
on submenu that appears.

*The **New Toolbar** dialog box appears.*

4 Select folder that you want to appear as a toolbar.

> ✓ *Click plus sign (+) to expand folders to view subfolders.*

5 Click 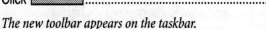 .... Enter

The new toolbar appears on the taskbar.

Move Toolbars Off Taskbar

1 Point to empty area on taskbar.

2 Drag toolbar off taskbar onto desired area of desktop.

The mouse pointer becomes a ⬚ to indicate that you are moving a toolbar.

continued...

THE DESKTOP

Move Toolbars Off Taskbar (cont.)

3 Release mouse button to drop toolbar onto desktop.

The toolbar appears with a title bar.

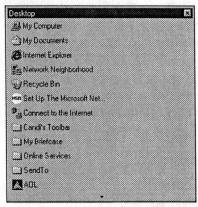

> 📖 *When you drag a toolbar to the edge of the screen, Windows 98 "docks" it by securing it in place. When you dock toolbars on the desktop, Windows 98 realigns icons on the desktop to fit within the desktop space.*

Delete Items on a Taskbar Toolbar

1 Right-click item you want to delete from toolbar.

2 Click **Delete** ....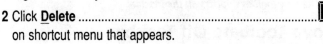
on shortcut menu that appears.

> 📖 *If you delete a special command, like the **Show Desktop** button on the **Quick Launch** toolbar, to restore it you can use the **Find** command to search for .scf files (type *.scf in the **Named** box), then drag the found item from the **Find** result window back onto the **Quick Launch** toolbar. See **Find Items on Your Computer,** page 147.*

SYSTEM MANAGEMENT

DISK MANAGEMENT

Windows 98 lets you copy and format floppy disks easily. You can also maintain your hard disk with Windows 98 tools.

Copy Floppy Disk

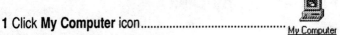 *From the Desktop*

1 Click **My Computer** icon .... My Computer

The My Computer window opens.

2 Right-click **floppy drive** icon ....
containing diskette to copy.

3 Click **Copy Disk** .... Y
on shortcut menu that appears.

The Copy Disk dialog box appears.

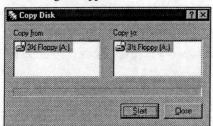

4 Select source disk in **Copy from** list box.

5 Select destination disk in **Copy to** list box.

> *If you have only one floppy drive, Windows 98 will automatically set the source and destination disks as the same disk drive.*

6 Insert disk in disk drive.

7 Insert destination disk at the prompt.

8 Click 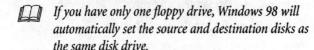 Start .... Alt + S

Windows 98 reads the source disk.

continued...

111

SYSTEM MANAGEMENT

Copy Floppy Disk (cont.)

9 Click `OK` .... `Enter`

Windows 98 writes the data to the destination disk.

10 Click `Close` .... `C`

when Windows 98 is finished copying to disk.

Format Floppy Disk

⑂ From the Desktop

1 Click **My Computer** icon .... `My Computer`

The My Computer window opens.

2 Right-click **floppy drive** icon ....
containing diskette to copy.

3 Click **For_mat** .... `M`
on shortcut menu that appears.

The Format Floppy Disk dialog box appears.

4 Select disk capacity from **Capacity** drop-down list box.

5 Select desired format type:

- **Quick (erase)** option button .... `Alt`+`Q`
  *to reformat disk quickly without checking
  for disk errors.*

- **Full** option button .... `Alt`+`F`
  to format or reformat disk and check for disk errors.

- **Copy system files only** option button .... `Alt`+`O`
  to transfer system files to formatted disk.

To label disk when formatting:

- Type desired label name .... *name*
  in **Label** text box.

112

SYSTEM MANAGEMENT

Format Floppy Disk (cont.)

To remove label when formatting:
- Select **No label** check box .... `Alt` + `N`

To report results of formatting when done:
- Select **Display summary** .... `Alt` + `D`
  when finished check box.

To make disk bootable after formatting:
- Select **Copy system files** check box .... `Alt` + `Y`

6 Click `Start` .... `Alt` + `S`

The Format Disk dialog box appears. Windows 98 will format the disk.

7 Click `Close` .... `Enter`
to exit **Format Results** dialog box.

8 Click `Close` .... `Esc`
to exit **Format Floppy Disk** dialog box.

View and Set Disk Properties

⌐ From the Desktop

1 Click **My Computer** icon .... My Computer
The My Computer window opens.

2 Right-click desired drive icon.

3 Click **Properties** .... `R`
on shortcut menu that appears.

The Properties dialog box appears.

To view drive information:
- Click **General** tab .... `Ctrl` + `Tab`

Windows shows the following drive information: Label, Type, File System, Used space, Free space, Capacity, and percentage of used and free space on the disk.

continued...

113

SYSTEM MANAGEMENT

Disk Properties (cont.)

To change the disk label:

a Click in **Label** text box.. `Alt` + `L`

b Type desired label name.. *name*

To run disk tools:

a Click **Tools** tab.. `Ctrl` + `Tab`

b Click `Check Now` .... `Alt` + `C`
to run ScanDisk. *See **ScanDisk**, below.*

c Click `Backup Now...` .... `Alt` + `B`
to start Backup. *See **Microsoft Backup**, page 118.*

d Click `Defragment Now...` .... `Alt` + `D`
to start Disk Defragmenter. *See **Disk Defragmenter**, page 117.*

4 Click `OK` .... `Enter`

ScanDisk

Use ScanDisk to check your hard disk for logical and physical errors.
ScanDisk can then repair the damaged areas.

1 Click `Start` .... 🔁

2 Point to **Programs** .... `Programs`

3 Point to **Accessories** .... `Accessories`

4 Point to **System Tools** .... `System Tools`

5 Click **ScanDisk** .... `ScanDisk`

The ScanDisk dialog box appears.

6 Select drive containing files and folders you want to check.

7 Select **Standard** option button .... `D`
to check folders and files for errors.

OR

Check **Thorough** option button .... `T`
to scan disk surface, as well as folders and files, for errors.

SYSTEM MANAGEMENT

ScanDisk (cont.)

8 Click to set other options, as desired:

- Click **Options** .... **O**

  to change settings ScanDisk uses when checking disk surface.

- Click **Advanced** .... **A**

  to change settings ScanDisk uses when
  checking files and folders.

- Deselect **Automatically fix errors** check box .... **F**

  if you want to specify how ScanDisk repairs errors it finds.

  ✓ *You can right-click options, and then click **What's***
    ***This?** on the shortcut menu that appears for Help with*
    ScanDisk options.

9 Click **Start** .... **S**

ScanDisk checks your folders, files, and/or drives for errors,
depending on the type of test you selected.

10 Click **Close** .... Enter

to exit **ScanDisk Results** dialog box.

11 Click **Close** .... Enter

to exit **ScanDisk** dialog box.

Disk Cleanup

*You can run **Disk Cleanup** to help free up space on your hard drive.*
Disk Cleanup searches your hard drive, and then lists temporary files,
Internet cache files, and unnecessary program files that you can safely
*delete. You can also run **Disk Cleanup** when viewing **Disk Properties***
*from the **General** tab by clicking **Disk Cleanup**. See **View and Set***
***Disk Properties**, page 113.*

1 Click **Start** ....

2 Point to **Programs** .... **Programs**

continued...

SYSTEM MANAGEMENT

Disk Cleanup (cont.)

3 Point to **Accessories**... 🏠 Accessories

4 Point to **System Tools**....................................... 🖥 System Tools

5 Click **Disk Cleanup**... 🗑 Disk Cleanup

The Select Drive dialog box appears.

6 Select drive you want to clean from **Drives** drop-down list.

7 Click [OK].. Enter

The Disk Cleanup dialog box appears with an estimate of how much disk space you can free up and a listing of the files you can delete to free up that disk space.

8 Select check box(es) next to file type to remove in **Files to delete** list box.

You can read a description of each file type in the Description area under the list.

To view files to be deleted:

a Select file type name.

b Click [View Files] to open folder containing selected files.

c Click close button [X] when done.

9 Click [OK].. Enter

Disk Cleanup asks you to confirm the file deletion.

10 Click [Yes] to delete selected files .... Enter

System Management

Disk Defragmenter

*You can use **Disk Defragmenter** to rearrange files and unused space on your hard disk so that programs run faster.*

> ✓ *You may want to disable your screen saver before beginning a defragmentation because Disk Defragmenter starts over each time the screen changes. If you choose not to disable your screen saver, the defragmentation process may take awhile.*

1 Click 🏁 Start .... 🗐

2 Point to **Programs** .... 📁 Programs

3 Point to **Accessories** .... 📁 Accessories

4 Point to **System Tools** .... 📁 System Tools

5 Click **Disk Defragmenter** .... 💿 Disk Defragmenter

*The **Select Drive** dialog box appears.*

6 Select drive you want to defragment from drop-down list.

7 Click ▓ OK ▓ .... Enter

*The **Defragmenting Drive** dialog box appears, and Windows 98 begins to defragment the chosen drive.*

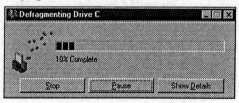

> 📖 *If Windows 98 tells you that your disk has errors that need to be fixed before the drive can be defragmented, click ▓ OK ▓, then run **ScanDisk**. Run a **Thorough** test and make sure the **Automatically fix errors** check box is selected.*

continued...

117

SYSTEM MANAGEMENT

Disk Defragmenter (cont.)

8 Click command buttons, as desired:

- **Stop** .... **Alt** + **S**

  stops the defragmention process.

- **Pause** .... **Alt** + **P**

  pauses the defragmention process so that you can perform other tasks without losing the progress you've made. When you click this button, it turns to **Resume** *which you can click to resume defragmentation.*

- **Show Details** .... **Alt** + **D**

  takes you into a larger window where you can view process details.

9 Click **Close** .... **Enter**

to exit Disk Defragmenter.

SYSTEM TOOLS AND SETTINGS

Microsoft Backup

You can use **Microsoft Backup** *to back up files on your hard disk. You can store these backup files on floppy disks, a tape drive, or another computer on your network. If your original files are damaged or lost, you can restore them from your backup copy.*

> 📖 *If you do not see* **Backup** *on the* **Accessories** *menu, it is not installed. See* **Add or Remove Windows Components***, page 50.*

1 Click **Start** .... 🔁

2 Point to **Programs** .... 📁 Programs

3 Point to **Accessories** .... 📁 Accessories

4 Point to **System Tools** .... 📁 System Tools

5 Click **Backup** .... 🔁 Backup

SYSTEM MANAGEMENT

Microsoft Backup (cont.)

*The **Microsoft Backup** welcome dialog box appears.*

If you select an option and click **OK** *, a wizard will walk you through the steps to carry out a backup or restore procedure.*

If you click **Close** *you can go to the **Microsoft Backup** program screen to perform backup procedures.*

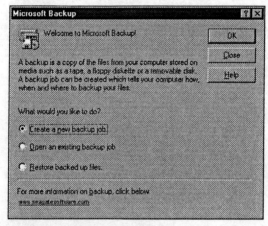

6 Select desired backup option button:

- **Create a new backup job**.................................**N**

- **Open an existing backup job**............................**O**

- **Restore backed up files**.....................................**R**

7 Click **OK** ....**Enter**

*Follow the wizard prompts for the option you selected. When you complete the process, the **Microsoft Backup** window will appear.*

SYSTEM MANAGEMENT

Microsoft Backup (cont.)

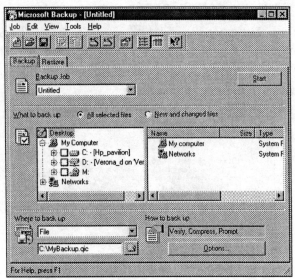

✓ *Rest the mouse pointer on a toolbar item to see its name.*

✓ *Click the **Backup Wizard** tool to back up files.*

✓ *Click the **Restore Wizard** tool to restore files you have backed up.*

✓ *Click the **Help** menu in the **Microsoft Backup** window for more information.*

Schedule Tasks

Windows 98 lets you schedule tasks (applications) so that they can run at a specified time automatically. For example, you might use this feature to schedule disk management tasks, such as ScanDisk, to run during your lunch break.

1 Click **My Computer** icon .... My Computer

SYSTEM MANAGEMENT

Schedule Tasks (cont.)

🔲
Scheduled
Tasks

2 Click **Scheduled Tasks** ....

The Scheduled Tasks window opens.

🔲
Add
Scheduled
Task

3 Click **Add Scheduled Task** icon ....

The Scheduled Task Wizard appears.

> 📖 *Other icons for system management tools may appear in the Scheduled Tasks window. Click the desired icon to start its tool.*

4 Click `Next >` .... `Alt` + `N`

5 Select program to schedule from list box.
OR

Click `Browse...` .... `Alt` + `R`
to locate application that is not in list.

6 Click `Next >` .... `Alt` + `N`

7 Type new program name ....*name*
if you want to schedule same task in several ways.

8 Select option button for how frequently you would like to perform the task.

9 Click `Next >` .... `Alt` + `N`

10 If prompted, select time and day you want task to start.
Options available depend on the selection made in step 8.

11 Click `Next >` .... `Alt` + `N`

Windows 98 confirms the tasks you have scheduled. If you want to make any changes, click `< Back` to move back through the Scheduled Task Wizard dialog boxes.

12 Click `Finish` .... `Enter`

121

SYSTEM MANAGEMENT

Set Mouse Properties

1 Click **Start** .... 📖

2 Point to **Settings** .... **Settings**

3 Point to **Control Panel** .... **Control Panel**

4 Click **Mouse** icon .... Mouse
   in **Control Panel** window.

5 Set desired properties as described in tables that follow.
   The options may vary depending on the mouse you have
   installed on your computer.

Buttons Tab

Button configuration	Select primary mouse button (Right-handed or Left-handed option button).
Double-click speed	Select time between sequence of clicks when double-clicking by moving slide bar.
Test area	Double-click icon to test double-click speed.

Pointers Tab

Scheme	Select a saved cursor pointer scheme from drop-down list.
Save As	Click to save current pointer settings as a scheme.
Delete	Click to delete selected pointer scheme.
Use Default	Click to use default pointer scheme.
Browse	Click to replace selected pointer with another pointer. (Pointers are stored in .cur files.)

SYSTEM MANAGEMENT

Mouse Properties (cont.)

Motion Tab

Pointer speed	Drag slide bar to change speed of pointer when moving mouse.
Show pointer trails	Select to show trail when moving mouse. Then, drag slider to adjust length of pointer trail.

6 Click .... `Enter`

Set System Performance Settings

You can view general information about your system, manage devices (enable, disable and set device properties), set up hardware profiles, and set performance options such as the use of virtual memory.

1 a Right-click **My Computer** icon............................... My Computer

  b Click **Properties**.. `R`
   on shortcut menu that appears.

OR

  a Click ....

  b Point to **Settings** .... Settings

  c Point to **Control Panel** .... Control Panel

  d Click **System** icon .... System
   in **Control Panel** window.

*The **System Properties** dialog box appears.*

2 Click desired tab... `Ctrl` + `Tab`

3 Set or view desired properties as described in lists that follow.

> 💣 *You should not change a system setting unless you completely understand the effect of the change. Consult hardware and software documentation for information.*

continued...

SYSTEM MANAGEMENT

System Performance Settings (cont.)

General Tab

System	Shows current version of Windows.
Registered to	Shows name of registered user.
Computer	Shows computer processor and total memory.

Device Manager Tab

View devices by type	Select to list devices by categories.
View devices by connection	Select to list devices by the hardware to which they are connected.
Hardware list	Select plus sign of device category or connection to view or edit, then click the device to select it.
Properties	Click to change or view properties of selected device.

General properties include:

- Information about the device.

- **Device usage** - select hardware profile for which device can be enabled or disabled.

📖 *Depending on the device in use, other property tabs may be available.*

Driver properties may include:

- Driver files
- Files details
- Change driver

SYSTEM MANAGEMENT

System Performance Settings (cont.)

Resource properties may include:

- Resource settings
  (e.g., IRQ/Memory Address)
- Use automatic settings
- Change Setting
- Conflicting device list

Refresh	Click to update list to show recent changes.
Remove	Click to remove selected device in hardware list.
Print	Click to print summary of devices and their properties.

Hardware Profiles Tab

📖 *Profiles let you start your computer with different hardware configurations.*

Profiles list	Shows hardware profiles (device settings) for your computer.
Copy	Click to copy selected profile to a new hardware profile. You can then select or deselect hardware devices for use with the profile.
Rename	Click to rename selected profile.
Delete	Click to delete selected profile.

Performance Tab

Performance status Memory	Shows total RAM for your computer.
System Resources	Shows percentage of free system resources.

continued...

SYSTEM MANAGEMENT

System Performance Settings (cont.)

File System	Shows type of file system in use.
Virtual Memory	Shows type of virtual memory in use.
Disk Compression	Shows type of disk compression in use.
PC Cards (PCMCIA)	Shows information about PC Cards in use.

Advanced settings

File System
- Hard Disk properties
- Typical role of this machine (Desktop computer, Mobile or docking system, Network server)
- Read-ahead optimization
- CD-ROM optimization
  - Supplemental cache size
  - Optimize access pattern for (speed of CD-ROM)

📖 *Options for this setting may vary.*

Graphics Select graphics hardware acceleration.

Virtual Memory Select these virtual memory properties:

- Let Windows manage my virtual memory settings (recommended)

- Let me specify my own virtual memory settings
  - Hard disk
  - Minimum
  - Maximum
  - Disable virtual memory (not recommended)

SYSTEM MANAGEMENT

Set Volume Control

You can control the audio volume for playback, recording, and other installed audio devices.

1 Click **sound** icon..
in taskbar notification area.

A volume control appears above the taskbar.

2 Drag slider up or down.

OR

Select **Mute** check box..

OPEN VOLUME CONTROL

*With **Volume Control**, you can:*

- *Control volume on installed sound devices.*

- *Control the balance between speakers on installed sound devices.*

- *Add and remove controls for audio devices.*

- *Mute one device while playing another to avoid mixing sounds.*

- *Mute all sound devices.*

- Double-click **sound** icon..
in taskbar notification area.

*The **Volume Control** dialog box appears.*

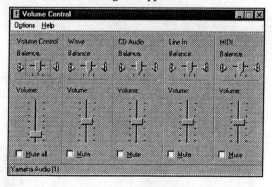

SYSTEM MANAGEMENT

Set Sound Properties

1 Click **Start** ....

2 Point to **Settings** .... Settings

3 Point to **Control Panel** .... Control Panel

4 Click **Sounds** icon .... Sounds
in **Control Panel** window.

*The **Sounds Properties** dialog box appears.*

5 Set desired properties as described in table that follows:

Sounds Tab

Events Area	Select event to assign sound to in Events list.
Sound Area	
Name	Select .wav file to assign to selected event in Name drop-down list.
Browse	Click to search for other .wav files to assign to selected event.
Details	Click to display properties of .wav file in Name drop-down list.
Preview	Click button to preview selected sound.
Schemes Area	Select named sound scheme from drop-down list.
Save As	Click to save current event assignments to a named scheme.
Delete	Click to delete selected scheme.

SYSTEM MANAGEMENT

UPDATE WINDOWS 98

Windows Update lets you download driver and system file updates from Microsoft's resource Web site. You can also receive up-to-date online technical support through Windows Update.

Open Windows Update

1 Click 🏁 Start .... 📖

2 Click **Windows Update** .... 🖥 Windows Update

> 📖 *You can also access Windows Update from the **Settings** submenu on the **Start** menu.*

Windows 98 connects to the Windows Update Web site.

> 📖 *The first time you use Windows Update, you might receive a dialog box requesting that you register your Windows 98 product.*

3 Click desired link on Windows Update Web site.

*You can select the link for the **Update Wizard** to download driver and system file updates for Windows 98.*

> 📖 *Microsoft updates the Windows Update Web site to keep it current, so it may look different each time you visit.*

Folders and Files

FOLDERS AND FILES

*A **folder** is a directory that holds other folders and files. When a folder is open, its contents appear in a window, as in the illustration below.*

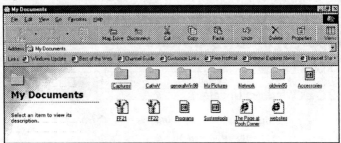

When closed, a folder is represented as a folder icon
Some special folders are represented by a folder with a picture
*on it   See **Folders and Files**, page 19.*

FOLDER TOOLBARS
Standard Folder Toolbar

Folder windows and Windows Explorer make use of a common toolbar. This toolbar contains buttons (tools) to help you work with files and folders.

Click:	To:
	Move back to previously viewed folder.
	Move forward to previously viewed folder.
	Open parent folder of the current folder.
	Move selected items to the clipboard.

FOLDERS AND FILES

Standard Folder Toolbar (cont.)

Click:	To:
Copy	Copy selected items to the clipboard.
Paste	Insert clipboard contents.
Undo	Cancel last action you performed.
Delete	Delete selected items.
Properties	Show or change properties of selected item.
Views	Change view of folder items.

*Folder windows and Windows Explorer also contain the **Address bar**, where you can enter a local file path or a Web address to go to the desired location.*

*See **Use Address Bar to Access a Web Site**, page 183, for more information on the **Address bar**.*

*The **Links bar** is also displayed by default in folder windows and the Windows Explorer window.*

*Use the **Links bar** to create and access shortcuts to Web addresses. See **Use Links Toolbar to Access the Web**, page 181.*

FOLDERS AND FILES

Hide or Show Folder Toolbars

1 Click **View** menu... Alt + V

2 Point to **Toolbars** .... T

3 Click to select/deselect desired toolbar
or toolbar feature:

- **Standard Toolbar** .... S

- **Address Bar**... A

- **Links Bar**... L

- **Text Labels** .... T

> ✓ *Consider hiding the **Text Labels** (the function names that appear on each toolbar button) to conserve space. Then, if you need to know the name of a button later, rest the pointer on the button and its name will appear.*

Access Internet Explorer Toolbar

1 Click **View** menu... Alt + V

2 Point to **Toolbars** .... T

3 Click desired **Explorer bar** to access Internet Explorer.

*See **Use Explorer Bars to Access a Web Site**, page 183.*

FOLDERS AND FILES

CUSTOMIZE FOLDER APPEARANCE
Folder Styles

*By default, Windows 98 uses the **Web browsing style** (single-click). If you wish, however, you can choose the **Classic browsing style** (double-click), or you can set up a **custom browsing style** that provides an appropriate mix of browsing features for your work style.*

Comparing Web and
Classic Browsing Options

The table below shows how folder options are affected by different browsing styles.

Folder Option	Web style	Classic style
Browsing	New windows open using the same window.	New windows open using separate windows.
Select	Point to an item.	Click an item.
Open	Click an item.	Double-click an item.
Back/Forward	Enabled.	Disabled.

Change Folder Browsing Style

☞ From the Start Menu

1 Click **Start** .... 🕮

2 Point to **Settings** .... 🕮 Settings

3 Click **Folder Options** .... F

continued...
133

FOLDERS AND FILES

Change Browsing Style (cont.)

*The **Folder Options** dialog box appears with **General** tab selected.*

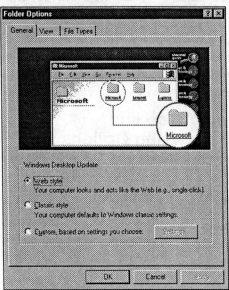

4 Select desired browsing style:

- **W**eb style .... W

  *(single-click) sets your computer to browse folders
  like Web pages.*

- **C**lassic style C

  *(double-click) sets your computer defaults
  to Windows classic settings.*

- C**u**stom, based on settings you choose .... U

  lets you set a mixture of Web and classic settings.

FOLDERS AND FILES

Change Browsing Style (cont.)

To create a custom folder browsing style:

a Click Settings... .... S

*The **Custom Settings** dialog box appears.*

b Select and/or click desired browsing options.

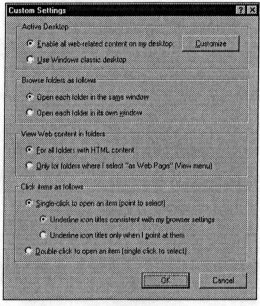

✓ *Click the Help button* ? *in the dialog box, then click the option you want help with.*

5 Click OK .... Enter

6 Click Close .... Enter

FOLDERS AND FILES

Change Folder View Settings

You can customize folder window settings.

1 Click **View** menu...`Alt`+`V`
   in a folder window.

2 Click **Folder Options** ....`O`

   *The **Folder Options** dialog box appears.*

3 Click **View** tab...`Ctrl`+`Tab`

4 Select or deselect desired check box option(s) in
   Advanced settings scroll box.

   ✓ *Click the Help button* `?` *in the dialog box, then click
   the option you want help with.*

5 Click command buttons as desired:

   ▪ `Like Current Folder` ....`Alt`+`L`

   to use the current folder settings for all folders.

   📖 *This option is not available if you open the **Folder
   Options** dialog box using the **Start** menu.*

   ▪ `Reset All Folders` ....`Alt`+`R`

   to reset all folders to Windows 98 default settings.

6 Click `OK` ....`Enter`

FOLDERS AND FILES

View a Folder as a Web Page

You can add a frame to the left side of the folder window to display information about selected items, including a thumbnail of selected graphic or HTML files.

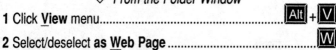

⌦ From the Folder Window

1 Click **View** menu..Alt + V

2 Select/deselect **as Web Page**..................................W

to turn the option on or off.

Customize Folders

*Windows 98 lets you customize most folders to look like a Web page. You cannot customize system folders, such as **My Computer** and **Recycle Bin**. Changing the folder background into an HTML document requires some knowledge of HTML. This book does not provide information on writing HTML code.*

Choose Folder Background Picture

⌦ From the Folder Window

1 Click **View** menu..Alt + V

2 Click **Customize this Folder**..................................C

*The **Customize this Folder Wizard** appears.*

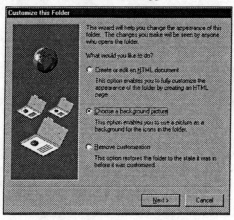

continued...

FOLDERS AND FILES
Folder Background (cont.)

3 Select **Choose a background picture** option button.......... C

4 Click `Next >` .... Alt + N

5 Select desired picture from the **Background picture for this folder** list.

   OR

   Click `Browse...` .... Alt + R

   to locate other background pictures on
   your computer. *See Use the Browse Button, page 146.*

6 Click `Next >` .... Alt + N

   Windows 98 lists the changes you have made.

7 Click `Finish` .... Enter

   📖 *If the changes you make do not appear, be sure to select
   the Web style browsing option. See Change Folder
   Browsing Style, page 133.*

Remove Folder Background Picture
✐ From the Folder Window

1 Click **View** menu... Alt + V

2 Click **Customize this Folder** C

   The Customize this Folder Wizard appears.

3 Select **Remove customization** option button..................... R

4 Click `Next >` .... Alt + N

   *Windows 98 will alert you that you are about to remove
   the customization from the folder.*

5 Click `Next >` .... Alt + N

   Windows lists the changes you have made.

6 Click `Finish` .... Enter

138

FOLDERS AND FILES

LOCATE FILES
Browse for Folders and Files
You can locate files on your computer by opening and browsing through folder windows or by using Windows Explorer to open folders from the hierarchy of folders in the left pane.

Browse Using Folder Windows

1 Set preferred browsing style, if you have not done so already. *See Change Folder Browsing Style, page 133.*

2 Click **My Computer** icon on desktop ....

The My Computer window opens.

3 Click desired drive icon...................... or or

A window displaying the selected drive's contents opens.

4 Click desired folder icon ....

A window displaying the contents of the selected folder opens.

5 Continue clicking folder icons until desired folder level appears.

The Address bar shows the path and name of the current folder.

✓ *You can enter a local, network, or Web address in the Address bar and then press* Enter *to go there quickly.*

6 Use the **Back, Forward,** and **Up** buttons to view folders you have opened previously. *See View Previously Opened Folders or Web Sites, page 141.*

7 Click desired folder or file icon to open it.

FOLDERS AND FILES

Browse Using Windows Explorer

*Windows Explorer is an application that lets you browse and manage all items in your computer from one central location. Windows Explorer is divided into the All Folders pane on the left and the Contents pane on the right. The **All Folders** pane shows the hierarchy of folders in your computer. The **Contents** pane shows the contents of the folder selected in the All Folders pane. Resize the panes by dragging the split bar.*

*In the **All Folders** pane:*
- *The desktop is the root folder from which all other folders can be accessed. Explorer shows the hierarchy of your folders below the **Desktop** folder.*

- *A + next to a folder indicates you can expand it to show its subfolders.*

- *A − next to a folder indicates you can collapse it to hide its subfolders.*
- *Folders without a + or − do not contain subfolders.*

*In the **Contents** pane:*
- *Explorer shows the contents of the selected folder.*

1 Select preferred browsing style if you have not done so already. *See **Change Folder Browsing Style**, page 133.*

2 Open **Windows Explorer**:

  a Click [🏁 Start] .... 🔳

  b Point to **P**rograms .... [🗒 Programs]

  c Click **Windows Explorer** .... [🖥 Windows Explorer]
OR

  a Right-click folder you want to explore.

  b Click **E**xplore .... [E]
    on shortcut menu that appears.

*The **Windows Explorer** window opens, displaying the contents of your computer. If you right-click a folder, that folder's contents appears in the Contents pane.*

FOLDERS AND FILES

Windows Explorer (cont.)

Windows Explorer options:

- Drag scroll bar in left pane if you want to view additional folders in the list.

- Click the **+** to the left of a folder in the left pane to see the folders it contains.

- Click the **-** to the left of a folder in the left pane to hide the folders it contains.

- Click desired folder in the left pane to view its content in the right pane.

- Click desired folder in the right pane to show its content in the right pane.

- Click desired folder or file icon in the right pane to open it in its own window.

View Previously Opened Folders or Web Sites

When browsing through folder windows, Windows Explorer, or the Internet, you can move up a level in the folder hierarchy or return to previously opened folders or Web sites.

GO UP ONE LEVEL IN HIERARCHY OF FOLDERS

- Click [⬆ Up] toolbar button .... [Backspace]

  *The **Up** button takes you to a local folder one level above the current folder. This button is dimmed if you are viewing the desktop, which is at the top of the hierarchy of folders.*

  OR

1 Click **Go** menu.. [Alt] + [G]
2 Click **Up One Level** .... [U]

141

Folders and Files

GO BACK TO PREVIOUS LOCATION

- Click 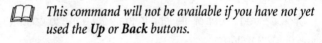 Back toolbar button.. `Alt` + `←`

    📖 *To use the **Back** and **Forward** buttons, you must enable Web style browsing. See **Change Folder Browsing Style**, page 133.*

    OR

1 Click **Go** menu.. `Alt` + `G`
2 Click **Back**... `B`

GO FORWARD TO PREVIOUS LOCATION

    📖 *This command will not be available if you have not yet used the **Up** or **Back** buttons.*

- Click 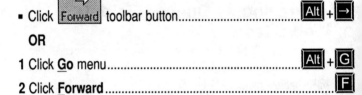 Forward toolbar button... `Alt` + `→`

    OR

1 Click **Go** menu.. `Alt` + `G`
2 Click **Forward**... `F`

FOLDERS AND FILES

Browse Using Common Dialog Boxes

Windows 98 provides common dialog boxes to help you browse folders when selecting, saving, and opening files on local and network drives. In these dialog boxes, you can also perform many file management tasks.

THE COMMON DIALOG BOX

Refer to the following illustration of the Open dialog box from WordPad for procedures on how to browse using common dialog boxes. Dialog boxes in other applications may have additional features.

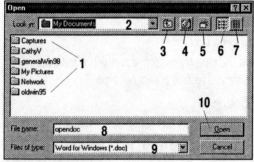

❶ folders and files list box

Double-click the folder or file to open it.

❷ Look in drop-down list

Click drop-down list to select a drive or folder from the hierarchy of folders in your computer.

❸ Up One Level button

Click button to select the parent folder of the current folder.

❹ View Desktop button

Click button to display items in the desktop folder (the top of the hierarchy of folders).

continued...

Folders and Files

Common Dialog Box (cont.)

❺ Create New Folder button

Click button to create a new folder in the current folder.

❻ List button

Click button to show files and folders in a list.

❼ Details button

Click button to show details of files and folders.

❽ File name text box

Type a filename using wildcards to limit the files displayed. For example, *help*.txt* will display all text files beginning with *help*.

❾ Files of type box

Select a file type from drop-down list to limit the files displayed to one particular type.

❿ Open button

Click button to open a selected folder or file.

MANAGE FILES IN COMMON DIALOG BOX

1 Right-click desired folder or file in **folders and files** list box.

2 Select desired option on shortcut menu that appears:

- **Select**...L
  opens the selected file.

- **Open**..O
  opens the selected file.

- **Print** (files only)............................P
  opens the program, prints the file, and closes the program again.

- **New** (files only) ....N
  creates a new copy of the selected document in the appropriate program.

FOLDERS AND FILES
Manage Files (cont.)

- **Quick View** (files only) .... [Q]

  *opens the Quick View window and lets you preview
  the file and make limited changes to it. See Preview Files,
  page 153.*

- **Send To** .... [T], [Enter]

  *sends the document to the destination you select.
  See Send Files to Other Destinations, page 172.*

- **Cut** .... [T], [Enter]

  *moves the contents of the selected folder or file
  to the clipboard. See Move or Copy Folders and
  Files, page 157.*

- **Copy** .... [C]

  *copies the contents of the selected folder a file
  to the clipboard. See Move or Copy Folders and
  Files, page 157.*

- **Create Shortcut** .... [S]

  *creates a shortcut to the selected folder or file.
  See Create Shortcuts, page 96.*

- **Delete** .... [D]

  *deletes the selected folder or file. See Delete
  Folders and Files, page 166.*

- **Rename** .... [M]

  *lets you modify the name of the selected folder or file.
  See Rename Folders and Files, page 159.*

- **Properties** .... [R]

  lets you view the properties for the selected folder or file.

FOLDERS AND FILES

Use the Browse Button

*Windows 98 gives you the option to use the **Browse** button to locate files from certain dialog boxes, including the **Run** command and **Find All Files**, **Create Shortcuts**, and **Install Program** dialog boxes.*

1 Click Browse...

📖 *The underlining in the button (Browse or Browse) will depend on which dialog box you are in.*

*The **Browse** dialog box appears.*

2 Select drive and/or folder containing desired file from **Look in** drop-down list.

3 Double-click subfolder in the folders and files list to open it, if necesary.

4 Select desired file in the folders and files list.

To change to the previous folder level:
- Click **Up** toolbar button... 🔼

To change to the Desktop folder:
- Click **Desktop** button... 🖊️

5 Click Open .... Alt + O

or appropriate button depending on your objective and the available commands.

*The **Browse** dialog box closes.*

FOLDERS AND FILES

Find Items on Your Computer

*Use the built-in **Find** utilities to search for files and folders on your computer, search for people and Web sites on the Internet, and search for computers on a network. You can work with found items immediately from the **Find** window. For example, you can open or print found documents, or you can drag found items to other folders.*

Find Folders and Files

You can search your computer for folders and files using search criteria that you assign.

> ✓ *Depending on how you open the **Find** dialog box, different locations appear in the **Look in** drop-down list box.*

> ✓ *If you select more than one search criteria (such as **Containing text** and a date range), Windows will find only items meeting all your criteria.*

> ✓ *If you click New Search, all search criteria is cleared. See **To clear current results and search criteria**, page 149.*

OPEN FIND ALL FILES DIALOG BOX

- Press **F3** F3

OR

- Press the **Windows** key while pressing **F** .... 🪟 + F

OR

1 Right-click folder icon you want to search.

2 Click <u>F</u>ind .... F
   on the shortcut menu that appears to search current folders.

OR

1 Click **Start** .... 🪟

continued...

FOLDERS AND FILES

Open Find All Files (cont.)

2 Point to **Find** .... 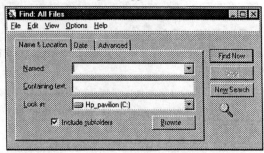 Find

3 Click **Files or Folders** .... Files or Folders...
to search **My Computer**.

The Find All Files dialog box appears.

FIND FOLDERS AND FILES BY NAME AND LOCATION

Search your computer for folders or files or that match the name and/or location you specify.

1 Open **Find All Files** dialog box. *See Open Find All Files Dialog Box, page 147.*

2 Type name to search for .... *name*
in the **Named** text box.

> *You can enter partial names, or you can select past search items from the **Named** drop-down list box.*

3 Click in **Look in** drop-down list box .... `Alt` + `L`

4 Type or select location to search .... *location*

To exclude subfolders from the search:
- Deselect **Include subfolders** check box .... `S`

5 Click `Find Now` .... `Alt` + `I`

Search results appear in a list box below the Find form.

FOLDERS AND FILES

Find Folders/Files (cont.)

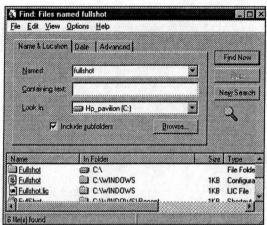

To stop a search:

- Click [Stop] .... `Alt` + `P`

To clear current results and search criteria:

a Click [New Search] .... `Alt` + `W`

A dialog box appears asking you to confirm your decision.

b Click [OK] to confirm .... `Enter`

*The **Find All Files** dialog box appears with a blank Find form so you can begin another search.*

To open a file or folder from the results list:

- Click desired folder or file.

OR

a Right-click desired folder or file.

b Click **Open**.. `O`
   on shortcut menu that appears.

OR

a Select desired file or folder.

continued...

FOLDERS AND FILES

Find Folders/Files (cont.)

  b Click **File** menu .... `Alt` + `F`

  c Click **Open** .... `O`

FIND FOLDERS OR FILES BY FILE TYPE

Search your computer for folders or files that match a specified file type.

  1 Open **Find All Files** dialog box. *See **Open Find All Files Dialog Box**, page 147.*

  2 Click **Advanced** tab .... `Ctrl` + `Tab`

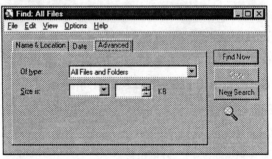

  3 Select folder or file type to search for from **Of type** drop-down list box.

  4 Click `Find Now` .... `Alt` + `I`

FIND FILES CONTAINING SPECIFIED TEXT

  1 Open **Find All Files** dialog box. *See **Open the Find All Files Dialog Box**, page 147.*

  2 Click **Name & Location** tab .... `Ctrl` + `Tab`

  3 Type text to search for .... *text* in **Containing text** box.

150

FOLDERS AND FILES

Find Files (cont.)

4 Click **Options** menu .... `Alt` + `O`

5 Select/deselect **Case Sensitive** .... `C`

📖 *If you select (add a check mark to) **Case Sensitive**, Windows will search for text exactly as you entered it. For example, if you entered "APRIL," Windows would only find files containing the word April in all uppercase letters.*

6 Click **Find Now** .... `Alt` + `I`

FIND FILES BY FILE SIZE

Search your computer for files that fall within a specified size range.

1 Open **Find All Files** dialog box. *See Open Find All Files Dialog Box, page 147.*

2 Click **Advanced** tab .... `Ctrl` + `Tab`

3 Type desired file size .... *number* in the **KB** text box.

4 Select **At least** on the **Size** is drop-down list to find files that are the same or greater than the size you entered.

OR

Select **At most** on the **Size** is drop-down list to find files that are the same or smaller than the size you entered.

5 Click **Find Now** .... `Alt` + `I`

151

FOLDERS AND FILES

FIND FILES BY DATE

You can search your computer for files that were created, modified, or opened within a specified range of dates.

1 Open **Find All Files** dialog box. *See **Open Find
All Files Dialog Box**, page 147.*

2 Click **Date** tab ....

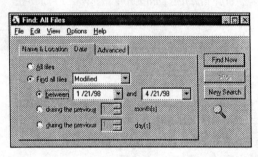

3 Select **Find all files** option button ....

4 Select desired date range:

- Select **between** option button and enter the first
  and last dates in the range you want to search within.

- Select **during the previous** option button and enter
  the number of months to search back through.

- Select **during the previous** option button and enter
  the number of days to search back through.

5 Click drop-down arrow and select desired search option:

- **Modified** to find files that were last modified
  within the specified date range.

- **Created** to find files created within the specified date range.

- **Last accessed** to find files last opened within the
  specified date range.

6 Click [Find Now] ....

FOLDERS AND FILES

Preview Files

*You can use the **Quick View** window to view the contents of files selected on the desktop, in a folder window, in the Windows Explorer contents pane, or in a common dialog box. If the **Quick View** command is not available, the data file type may not be supported or you may need to install the **Quick View** component of Windows 98. See **Add or Remove Windows Components**, page 50.*

OPEN QUICK VIEW USING SHORTCUT MENU

1 Right-click file you want to preview.

2 Click **Quick View**... Q

on shortcut menu that appears.

*The **Quick View** window appears showing the content(s) of the selected file.*

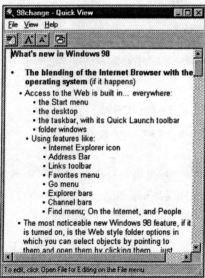

continued...

FOLDERS AND FILES

Open Quick View (cont.)

3 Use **Quick View** toolbar buttons to execute desired commands:

Opens the file you are previewing so that you can edit it. The button will look like the icon for the file's original application.

Increases the font size of the file.

Decreases the font size of the file.

Sets Quick View to open the next file you preview in the same window.

OPEN QUICK VIEW USING FOLDER WINDOW MENU

1 Select file to preview.

2 Click **File** menu..`Alt`+`F`

3 Click **Quick View**...`Q`

*The **Quick View** window appears showing the content(s) of the selected file.*

PREVIEW A FILE BY DRAGGING

*You can open a new file for viewing in the already opened **Quick View** window.*

- Drag desired file icon onto **Quick View** window.

*The **Quick View** window displays the contents of the dragged file.*

FOLDERS AND FILES

USE VIEW MENU IN QUICK VIEW WINDOW

*The **View** menu contains additional useful options. Some of the options listed below, however, may be dimmed depending on the file you are previewing.*

☞ *On the File Menu*

Click:	**To:**
Open File for Editing	Open the file you are previewing so you can make edits.
Exit	Close the Quick View window.

☞ *On the View Menu*

Click:	**To:**
Toolbar	Show or hide the toolbar.
Status Bar	Show or hide the status bar.
Page View	Switch the preview mode between Document and Page View.

📖   *Page View mode provides tabs in the page corner to view other pages. See the illustration, page 156.*

Replace Window	Set Quick View to display subsequent file selections in the same window.
Landscape	Switch the page view between Portrait and Landscape.
Rotate	Turn graphic files horizontally when Page View is deselected.
Font	Set the font for previewing text files.

continued...

FOLDERS AND FILES
View Menu in Quick View (cont.)

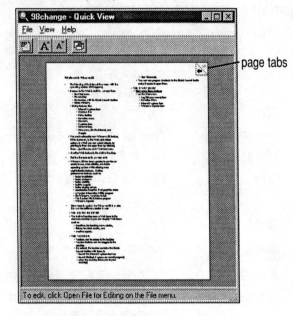

page tabs

FOLDERS AND FILES

MANAGE FOLDERS AND FILES
Move or Copy Folders and Files Using Menu

1 Select folders or files you want to move or copy.
*See **Select Folders and Files**, page 166.*

To move selected items:

a Click **Edit** menu... `Alt`+`E`

b Click **Cut**.. `T`

The cut file's icon will be dimmed.

To copy selected items:

a Click **Edit** menu... `Alt`+`E`

b Click **Copy**.. `C`

2 Open destination folder window.

3 Click **Edit** menu... `Alt`+`E`

4 Click **Paste**.. `P`

FOLDERS AND FILES

Move or Copy Folders and Files by Dragging

> *The icon of the item(s) you are draging will indicate a copy operation with a + sign. By default, items dragged between folders on the same drive are moved, and items dragged to a folder on another drive are copied.*

1 Arrange desktop so source folder and destination folder windows (or icons) are in view.

2 Select items to move or copy. *See **Select Folders and Files**, page 166.*

To move items:

- Press **Shift**.. `Shift`
  and drag selected items onto destination folder window.

To copy items:

- Press **Ctrl**.. `Ctrl`
  and drag selected items onto destination folder window.

To undo a copy:

a Right-click any blank area of any folder.

b Click **Undo Copy** .... `U`
  on shortcut menu that appears.

FOLDERS AND FILES

Rename Folders and Files

You can rename folders and files on the desktop, in a folder window, in the Windows Explorer contents pane, or in a common dialog box.

✓ *Press* **F2** *to quickly rename selected folders or files.*

RENAME FOLDERS AND FILES BY RIGHT-CLICKING

1 Right-click folder or file to rename.

2 Click **Rename** .... **M**

on shortcut menu that appears.

Windows 98 highlights the name.

3 Edit or type folder/file name as desired ....*name*

4 Click on blank area of the workspace.

OR

Press **Enter** .... Enter

RENAME FOLDERS AND FILES USING MENU

📖 *You cannot use this method to rename items on the desktop.*

1 Select folder or file you want to move. *See **Select Folders and Files**, page 166.*

2 Click **File** menu .... **Alt** + **F**

3 Click **Rename** .... **M**

Windows 98 highlights the name.

4 Type or edit folder/file name as desired ....*name*

5 Click on blank area of the workspace.

OR

Press **Enter** .... Enter

FOLDERS AND FILES

Special Folders

Special folders are default folders created by Windows 98 that offer quick and easy file storage and access.

Group folders are folders within the **Start** menu folder that hold groups of program shortcuts and other folders. They represent menu items that appear in the **Programs** menu.

The **History folder** is located in the Windows folder and holds a list of Web sites that you have visited recently.

The **Subscriptions folder** is located in the Windows folder and contains your subscriptions to Web sites. See **Subscriptions**, page 190.

The **Favorites folder** holds frequently used Web addresses or computer locations for easy access. See **Favorites Folder**, page 193.

FOLDERS AND FILES

My Briefcase

My Briefcase synchronizes files that you've worked on from different computers (e.g., your home computer and your office computer), ensuring that you always have the most current version of the files you store in it.

OPEN MY BRIEFCASE

- Click **My Briefcase** icon.. My Briefcase
  on desktop.

  The My Briefcase folder window opens.

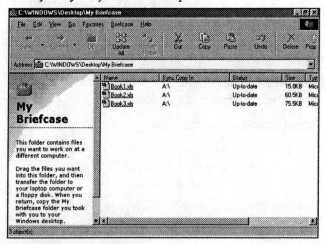

CREATE NEW BRIEFCASE

1 Right-click an empty area on desktop or in folder window.

2 Point to **New** ....

3 Click **Briefcase** .... Briefcase
  on shortcut menu that appears.

FOLDERS AND FILES

BRIEFCASE MENU COMMANDS

Briefcase folder windows also contain menus common to all folders in Windows 98. Those menu items are not covered in this table.

Click:	To:
Update All	Update all files in the Briefcase folder.
Update Selection	Updates selected files in the Briefcase folder.
Split From Original	Splits selected file so it can be worked with separately.

KEEP YOUR BRIEFCASE ON A FLOPPY DISK

☞ *From Your Main Computer*

1 Drag files you want to take on the road .... My Briefcase
onto **Briefcase** icon on the desktop.

2 Drag **Briefcase** onto floppy disk.

📖 *If you do additional work on the files from your main computer, open the* **Briefcase** *on the floppy disk and click the* **Update All** *toolbar button.*

Windows 98 will update the files in your Briefcase.

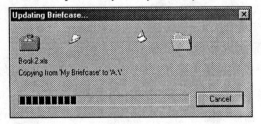

FOLDERS AND FILES

Briefcase on Floppy Disk (cont.)

✐ When on the Road

3 Open **Briefcase** on the floppy disk.

4 Drag files to a folder on your other computer's hard disk.

   ✓   *Leave the **Briefcase** on the floppy disk.*

✐ When You Finish Working with Files

5 Open **Briefcase** on the floppy disk.

6 Select **Update All** toolbar button ....

✐ When You Get Back to Your Computer

7 Open **Briefcase** on the floppy disk.

8 Select **Update All** command ....

My Documents

My Documents is a desktop folder that provides a place to store documents. Windows 98 accessory programs, such as WordPad, Notepad, and Paint, automatically store documents in the My Documents folder unless you change the save location.

OPEN MY DOCUMENTS

- Click **My Documents** icon .... My Documents
  on the desktop.

  OR

1 Click 🅑 Start ....

2 Point to <u>D</u>ocuments .... 📁 Documents

3 Click **My Documents** .... My Documents

FOLDERS AND FILES

SAVE A FILE IN MY DOCUMENTS

- Select **My Documents** in **Save in** text box of **Save As** dialog box. *See Save Files from a Windows Application, page 169.*

WORK WITH FOLDERS AND FILES
Create Folder by Right-Clicking

You can create a folder or file on the desktop, in a folder window, and in a common dialog box.

1 Right-click empty area on desktop, folder window, or common dialog box.

2 Point to **New** .... N

3 Click **Folder** .... F

A new folder icon appears with a temporary filename selected.

4 Type new folder name .... *name*

5 Press **Enter** .... Enter

   OR

   Click anywhere away from new folder name.

Create Folder Using Menu

1 Click **File** menu .... Alt + F

2 Point to **New** .... N

3 Click **Folder** .... F

A new folder icon appears with a temporary file name selected.

4 Type new folder name .... *name*

5 Press **Enter** .... Enter

Create File by Right-Clicking

1 Right-click empty area on desktop, in folder window, or in common dialog box.

2 Point to **New** .... N

3 Click desired file type on bottom of submenu.

> 📖 *File types for registered applications automatically appear on this menu.*

A file icon appears with a temporary filename selected.

4 Type or edit filename .... *name*

> 📖 *Press ← to edit the filename. To retain the association with the open application, do not change file extension.*

5 Press **Enter** .... Enter

OR

Click anywhere away from new file name.

Create File Using Menu

1 Click **File** menu .... Alt + F

2 Point to **New** .... N

3 Click desired file type on bottom of submenu.

> 📖 *File types for registered applications automatically appear on this menu.*

A file icon appears with a temporary filename selected.

4 Type or edit filename .... *name*

> 📖 *Press ← to edit the filename. To retain the association with the open application, do not change the file extension.*

5 Press **Enter** .... Enter

OR

Click anywhere away from new file name.

FOLDERS AND FILES

Delete Folders and Files

*When you delete folders and files from your hard disk, they are sent to the **Recycle Bin**. See **The Recycle Bin**, page 25.*

💣 *When you delete a folder, all its contents are deleted.*

1 Select folder or file to delete. *See **Select Folders and Files**, below.*

2 Press **Delete** .... `Delete`

   OR

   a Right-click the folder or file you want to delete.

   b Click **Delete** .... `D`
   on shortcut menu that appears.

Select Folders and Files

*With Windows 98, you can choose how to select folders and files by setting your preferred browsing style. See **Change Folder Browsing Style**, page 133.*

SELECT FOLDERS AND FILES USING
WEB BROWSING STYLE

- Point to item to select it.

   To select multiple consecutive items:
   Press **Shift** and point to last item in group .... `Shift`
   you want to select.

   To select multiple nonconsecutive items:
   Press **Ctrl** and point to items... `Ctrl`
   you want to select.

FOLDERS AND FILES

SELECT FOLDERS AND FILES USING
CLASSIC BROWSING STYLE

- Click item to select it.

  To select multiple consecutive items:
- Press **Shift** and click last item in group ....
  you want to select.

  To select multiple nonconsecutive items:
- Press **Ctrl** and click items... Ctrl
  you want to select.

Open Folders or Files

⌐ With Web Browsing Style

- Click selected item.

⌐ With Classic Browsing Style

- Double-click selected item.

⌐ With Either Browsing Style

- Press **Ctrl** while pressing **O**....................................... Ctrl + O

OR

1 Click **File** menu... Alt + F

2 Select **Open**... O

*The **Open** dialog box appears.*

3 Select drive containing file you want to open
from **Look in** drop-down list box.

4 Select folder containing desired file
from folders and files list.

5 Double-click subfolder in folders and files list to
open it, if necessary.

6 Select desired file in folders and files list.

7 Click .... Enter

167

FOLDERS AND FILES

OPEN FILE USING START MENU

*The **Documents** folder stores files you have recently opened.*

1 Click ![Start] .... 🗐

2 Point to **Documents** .... 📁 Documents

3 Select document to open from submenu that appears.

Windows 98 opens the file using the application in which it was created.

OPEN FILE BY RIGHT-CLICKING

1 Right-click icon for file you want to open.

2 Click **Open** .... O

on shortcut menu that appears.

OR

a Click **Open With** .... E

on shortcut menu that appears.

b Select application that will open the file from list box.

c Click [OK] .... Enter

OPEN FILE BY DRAGGING

1 Arrange desktop so document icon and destination application icon are in view.

2 Drag file icon onto desired application icon.

FOLDERS AND FILES

OPEN FOLDERS OR FILES USING RUN COMMAND

1 Click 🏁 Start .... 🎴

2 Click **Run** .... ⏳ Run...

*The **Run** dialog box opens.*

3 Type file path and name ....*path\name*
of file you want to open.

OR

Click **Open** down arrow and select recently used file
path and name.

OR

Click Browse... .... Alt + B
to locate and select file. *See **Use Browse Button**, page 146.*

4 Click OK .... Enter

Save Files from Windows Application

📖 *These are general procedures that apply to most
Windows-based applications. For further information,
refer to the specific application's documentation.*

SAVE FILE AS

*You can save a copy of an existing file with a new name and/or in a
new location.*

1 Click **File** menu .... Alt + F

2 Click **Save As** .... A

*The **Save As** dialog box displays.*

3 Select drive where you want to save file from **Save in**
drop-down list.

4 Select folder where you want to save the new file
in the folders and files list.

continued...

FOLDERS AND FILES

Save File As (cont.)

To change to the previous folder level:

- Click **Up** button...

To change to the desktop folder:

- Click **Desktop** button...

To create a new folder:

- Click **Create New Folder** button ....

5 Type new filename..*name*
   in **File name** text box.

6 Click ....

The file is saved to the location you specified. Each time you select
Save on the File menu, the file will be updated with whatever
changes you have made.

SAVE FILE

Save a file using its existing file name. If this is the first time you have
saved the file, you will be prompted for a file name and folder location.
See Save File As, page 169, steps 3-6.

1 Press **Ctrl** and **S**...

   OR

   a Click **File** menu ....

   b Click **Save** ....

2 If prompted for a filename, refer to **Save File As**, page 169,
   steps 3-6.

FOLDERS AND FILES

Print Files

When you print a file, Windows 98 sends it to your default printer unless you specify another printer.

PRINT OPEN FILE USING MENU

1 Click **File** menu .... `Alt` + `F`

2 Click **Print** .... `P`

*The **Print** dialog box opens.*

3 Set options in **Print** dialog box. *See **Customize Printer Settings**, page 229.*

4 Click [OK] .... `Enter`

PRINT CLOSED FILE BY DRAGGING

1 Open folder containing file you want to print.
*See **Open Folders or Files**, page 167.*

2 Arrange the desktop so that file and printer icons
(in **Printers** folder) are in view.

3 Drag file icon onto printer icon.

PRINT STORED FILES IN OFFLINE PRINTER QUEUE

This option is available for network printers or printers on some portable computers.

1 Open the **Printers** folder. *See **Open Printers Folder**, page 224.*

2 Right-click icon of printer that is set as offline.

3 Deselect **Work Offline** .... `W`
option on shortcut menu that appears.

171

FOLDERS AND FILES

Send Files to Other Destinations

THE SEND TO COMMAND

The Send To command lets you quickly send files to destinations such as a floppy disk, a mail recipient, a printer, or another folder.

1 Open folder containing folder or file to send.

2 Right-click item to send.

3 Point to **Send To** .... T
on shortcut menu that appears.

4 Click desired file destination on submenu that appears.

By default, the following destination shortcuts will appear on the Send To menu:

- *Floppy A*
- *Desktop as Shortcut*
- *Mail Recipient*
- *My Briefcase*
- *My Documents*

LOCATE AND ADD SHORTCUTS TO SENDTO FOLDER

When you add a shortcut to the SendTo folder, it creates a destination on the Send To menu.

1 Open **Find All Files** dialog box. *See **Open Find All Files Dialog Box**, page 147.*

2 Type *sendto* in **Named** text box ....*sendto*

3 Click Find Now .... Alt + I

4 Click the **SendTo** folder that appears in the result list.

FOLDERS AND FILES
Locate/Add Shortcuts (cont.)

5 Create desired shortcut in **SendTo** folder.
See Create Shortcuts, page 96.

The created shortcut will appear on the Send To submenu the next time you open it.

✓ *You can drag the SendTo folder onto the desktop from the result list in the Find All Files dialog box. This creates a shortcut to the SendTo folder on the desktop. Then you can add items to the Send To menu by dragging them onto the desktop shortcut.*

PRINT CLOSED FILE USING SEND TO COMMAND

1 Open folder containing file you want to print.

2 Right-click file icon.

3 Point to **Send To** .... 🔳
on shortcut menu that appears.

📖 *If the desired printer does not appear on the Send To menu, you can create a shortcut (see Create Shortcuts, page 96) to that printer in the SendTo folder. The printer will then appear as an option on the Send To menu.*

4 Click destination printer's icon ....

FOLDERS AND FILES

File Extensions

You can identify a document's file type by its icon and extension. The following table contains just a few of the file types you might find on your computer:

File Icon:	Type:	Extension:
	Bitmap image	.bmp
	GIF image	.gif
	Font file	.fon
	Generic icon	[varies]
	Help file	.hlp
	HTML document	.htm or .html
	MIDI sequence	.mid
	WAV file	.wav
	Execution file	[varies]
	Text file	.txt

File Extensions (cont.)

File Icon:	Type:	Extension:
	TrueType font file	.ttf
	Microsoft Word document	.doc

CHANGE FILE TYPES

You can change the application that starts when you open files of a certain type (files having a specific filename extension). For example, you might use this feature to have bitmap image files open in an advanced graphics program, rather than in the program that Windows assigns by default, Microsoft Paint.

1 Open any folder window.

2 Click **View** menu .... **Alt** + **V**

3 Click **Folder Options** .... **O**

*The **Folder Options** dialog box opens.*

4 Click **File Types** tab .... **Ctrl** + **Tab**

5 Select file type that you want to change in list box.

*The extension for the selected file type and the application that opens it appear in the **File type details** section.*

6 Click **Edit...** .... **Alt** + **E**

*The **Edit File Type** dialog box opens.*

7 Select **open** in **Actions** list box.

8 Click **Edit...** .... **Alt** + **E**

*The **Editing Action for Type** dialog box opens.*

continued...

FOLDERS AND FILES
Change File Types (cont.)

9 Type path and filename ....*path\name*
   of application you want to open whenever
   you open the selected file type.

   OR

   Click Browse.. ....**Alt**+**R**

   to locate the application you want to use.
   *See **Use the Browse Button**, page 146.*

10 Click OK ....**Enter**

   to close the **Editing Action for Type** dialog box.

11 Click Close to close **Edit File Type** dialog box.

12 Click Close to close **Folder Options** dialog box.

INTERNET TOOLS

ABOUT INTERNET TOOLS

Windows 98 provides numerous tools to access and browse the Internet. Windows 98 accessories and folder windows let you link to the World Wide Web directly from applications and your desktop.

Internet Definitions

Internet or World Wide Web (WWW)	Network of millions of computers that provide Web content, usually in the form of HTML (HyperText Markup Language).
browser	Program that lets you navigate on the Internet and view Web documents.
URL (Uniform Resource Locator)	Address that identifies a Web site location.
hyperlinks	Items embedded in documents that you click in order to go to another site, either on the Internet or on your computer. **Links** are graphics or words that appear in a different color and/or are underlined.
e-mail	Method of sending information from one computer to another across the Internet or a network; e-mail may contain text, files, and graphic backgrounds.
e-mail address	Notation that identifies an e-mail recipient and his or her domain location, such as *MikeS@msn.com*.
newsgroup	Method of exchanging information about a particular subject.

INTERNET TOOLS

Internet Utilities

1 Click **Start**

2 Point to **Programs**

3 Point to **Internet Explorer**

4 Click desired Internet utility:

With this utility:	You can:
	Store e-mail, home and work addresses and phone and fax numbers. Find addresses on the Internet using preinstalled directory services. Import addresses from other contact systems.
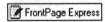	Set up or configure an Internet account.
	Edit and create HTML documents, including graphics, text, and links, that you can publish on the Internet, or on a local Intranet. Apply HTML tags, such as links, without typing the code. Save Web documents to the Web when Web Publishing Wizard is installed.
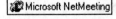	Have real-time conversation in a comic-strip environment over the Internet.
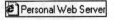	Collaborate with others in shared applications, file transfers, and chat messages.
Personal Web Server	Host and administer a Web site on your own computer (as part of an intranet), or develop and test a Web site before downloading it to an Internet service provider (ISP) for publication on the Internet.

INTERNET TOOLS

Internet Utilities (cont.)

Web Publishing Wizard	Upload Web page content to a Web server.
Windows Update...	Download the latest drivers and Windows components to keep your system up to date.

📖 *You can find the **Windows Update Wizard** on the **Start** menu.*

ACCESS THE INTERNET WITH WEB INTEGRATION

Windows 98 provides views of both local and Internet content. You can use common elements in the Windows environment, such as the desktop, taskbar, folder windows, and Windows Explorer, to view and work with Internet or local resources.

Use Active Desktop to Display Web Content

*Place active content, such as news, stock tickers, search windows, and standard Web pages on the desktop. Most Active Desktop features require access to the Internet. See **The Active Desktop**, page 74.*

continued...

INTERNET TOOLS

Active Desktop (cont.)

With the Active Desktop, you can:

❶ Create or save an HTML document (a Web page) and select it as your desktop background. You can click any links it may contain to go to a Web site quickly or send e-mail. *See Change Desktop Background, page 82.*

❷ Use Channel data as a screen saver. *See Change Desktop Screen Saver, page 86.*

❸ Type or select a Web address in the Address bar on the taskbar to open Internet Explorer and the selected Web site in one step. *See Customize Taskbar Toolbars, page 108.*

Use Channels to View Web Content

*Channels let you view Web content that is "pushed" to your computer in a stream. The **Channel bar** may appear on your desktop, if Active Desktop is enabled. See **View Channels**, page 71, and **Display Channel Bar on Desktop**, page 69.*

Use Folder Windows to Browse Web Content

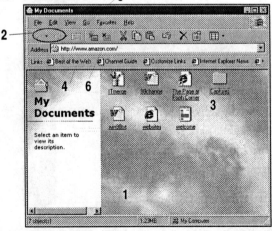

INTERNET TOOLS

Browse Web Content (cont.)

☞ From Any Folder Window:

❶ Customize folder to include background images, or edit HTML code for the folder window to include links, just like a Web page. *See Customize Folders, page 137.*

❷ Select Web style browsing to single-click items to open them, and use **Back** and **Forward** buttons on folder toolbars to navigate as you would in an Internet browser. *See Change Folder Browsing Style, page 133.*

❸ Drag link from a Web page onto folder window or desktop to create a shortcut to a Web site. Later, click shortcut to open Web site in one step. *See Create Shortcuts, page 96.*

❹ Add **Links** toolbar to folder window or taskbar, then click link to access Web site directly from folder window. *See Customize Taskbar Toolbars, page 108.*

❺ Click **Go** menu to access local computer or Web site. *See Use the Go Menu to Access a Site, page 182.*

❻ Type Web or local computer file location in folder or taskbar **Address bar** to view Web or local content in the same folder window. *See Use Address Bar to Access a Web Site, page 183.*

USE LINKS TOOLBAR TO ACCESS THE WEB

Open important Web sites without first opening Internet Explorer. To view the Links toolbar, see Hide or Show Folder Toolbars, page 132.

- Click desired link on **Links** toolbar to go to a link quickly.

OR

Add new links to **Links** toolbar by dragging **Address bar** icon, or a link on a Web page, onto **Links** toolbar.

INTERNET TOOLS

USE GO MENU TO ACCESS A SITE

Gain quick access to important Web and local computer sites quickly.

1 Click **Go** menu .... `Alt` + `G`

2 Click desired destination:

- **Home Page** .... `H`

  takes you to your selected Internet start page.

- **Search the Web** .... `S`

  *takes you to your selected Internet search engine
  (e.g., AOL NetFind).*

- **Channel Guide** .... `G`

  takes you to Active Channel Guide.

- **Mail** .... `M`

  *takes you to your selected Internet e-mail program
  (e.g., Outlook Express).*

- **News** .... `N`

  *takes you to your selected newsreader program
  (e.g., Outlook Express).*

- **My Computer** .... `C`

  takes you to My Computer folder.

- **Address Book** .... `A`

  *takes you to your specified contact or address
  book program (e.g., Microsoft Address Book).*

- **Internet Call** .... `I`

  *takes you to your specified Internet call program
  (e.g., Microsoft NetMeeting).*

INTERNET TOOLS

USE ADDRESS BAR TO ACCESS A SITE

You can go to both Web sites and locations on your computer with the Address bar. See Open Web Site Using Address Bar, page 189.

- Type desired address in **Address bar** ....*address*

  OR

  Click drop-down arrow on right side of **Address bar** to select a site you have recently visited from a list.

USE EXPLORER BARS TO ACCESS A WEB SITE

You can go to selected Web sites and locations on your computer with Explorer bars.

- Click desired **Explorer bar**................ button on Internet Explorer **Standard** toolbar.

  OR

1 Click **View** menu.. Alt + V
  in any folder window.

2 Select **Explorer bar**... E

  > *The active Explorer bar tool appears highlighted on the toolbar. To close the active Explorer bar, click the highlighted toolbar button.*

3 Select desired **Explorer bar** view:

- **Search Bar** .... S

  lets you specify search criteria for Internet sites in the left pane. Found items also appear in the left pane. When you select a found item, that Web page appears in the right pane. You can also choose a search provider in the drop-down list box, and utilize special features of the search provider that appears.

continued...
183

INTERNET TOOLS

Use Explorer Bars (cont.)

- **_F_avorites Bar** .... **F**

    lets you select Web sites or locations on your computer that you have added to your list of favorites. See **Favorites Folder,** *page 193.*

- **_H_istory Bar** .... **H**

    lets you select from Web sites you have visited previously.

- **_C_hannel Bar** .... **C**

    lets you view Web content that is "pushed" to your computer when you select a channel. See **Use Channels,** *page 69.*

INTERNET TOOLS

SET UP ONLINE SERVICES

Online services typically provide Internet access, special-interest forums, e-mail, information resources, and chat services.

Launch Internet Service Provider Software

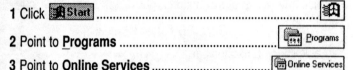

1 Click **Start**

2 Point to **Programs**

3 Point to **Online Services**

4 Click desired online service to install.

5 Follow the prompts as instructed.

INTERNET EXPLORER

Internet Explorer, Microsoft's Web browser program, is an integrated component of the Windows 98 operating system. With Explorer, you can access, browse, and download information from the Internet.

To use Internet Explorer, you must have an Internet connection, either through a modem line and an Internet service provider (ISP), or through a local area network.

> When you first start Internet Explorer, the **Connection Wizard** will open and walk you through the steps needed to set up a new Internet account. The **Connection Wizard** is also able to help you configure an existing Internet account if necessary.

INTERNET TOOLS

Start Internet Explorer

✑ From the Desktop

- Click **Internet Explorer** icon..

✑ From the Quick Launch Taskbar Toolbar

- Click **Internet Explorer** button..

✑ From Any Folder Window

- Click link on **Links** toolbar.

 OR

 Type or select Web address in **Address bar**.

 OR

 Select favorite Web site from folder's **Favorites** menu. *See **Open a Favorite**, page 193.*

 OR

 a Click **Go** menu...

 b Click **Home Page** ....

INTERNET TOOLS

The Internet Explorer Screen

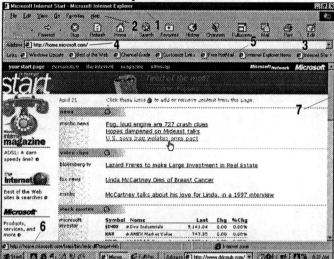

Below is a description of the tools available from the Explorer screen.

❶ title bar — Displays program name and current Web page.

❷ menu bar — Contains Internet Explorer command menus.

❸ Standard toolbar — Displays buttons for common tasks, such as loading, moving between, and printing Web pages.

❹ Address bar — Displays electronic address (URL) of current Web page (or file path if current document is a local file on your computer).

❺ Links bar — Contains links to various Microsoft sites and any sites you add to it.

❻ Status bar — Displays status of current link or download. When you place mouse pointer over a hyperlink, the Status bar displays the link's URL.

❼ scroll bars — Click scroll arrows or drag scroll bars to move screen view horizontally or vertically.

INTERNET TOOLS

Internet Explorer Standard Toolbar

 Moves you back through previously viewed sites.

 Moves you forward through previously viewed sites.

 Interrupts the current download.

 Reloads the current page.

 Brings you to your Home page.

 Opens Explorer bar, where you can select from a number of search services to find information on the Web.

 Opens Explorer bar and displays the Web sites you have stored using the tools in Favorites menu. *See Favorites Folder, page 193.*

 Opens Explorer bar and displays links to Web sites you have visited in previous days and weeks. Click again to close Explorer bar.

 Displays the list of current channels in the Explorer bar. Click again to close the Explorer bar. *See Use Channels, page 69.*

 Conceals menu bar, text titles, Status bar, and Address bar to utilize as much screen space as possible. Click again to return to normal view.

 Displays a menu of e-mail commands. *See Outlook Express, page 196.*

INTERNET TOOLS

Internet Explorer Toolbar (cont.)

Sends copy of the current page to your printer.

Opens copy of the current page in FrontPage Express, where you can edit and save it.

Open a Web Site Using Address Bar

1 Type **URL** in **Address bar**...*address*

2 Press **Enter**.. Enter

> 📖 *If you have visited the site before, Internet Explorer will try to guess the full address before you finish entering it in the **Address bar**. If the suggested address is correct, press* Enter *to go to it. If it is incorrect, continue typing over the suggestion with the desired URL.*

Internet Explorer connects to and displays the specified site.

Search the Web Using Internet Explorer Main Search Page

1 Start Internet Explorer. *See **Start Internet Explorer**, page 186.*

2 Click **Search** button on **Standard** toolbar.......................

   OR

   a Click **Go** menu.. Alt + G

   b Click **Search the Web**... S

*The **Explorer bar** opens on the left side of the screen with a search provider selected.*

3 Type search topic in text box....................................*keyword(s)*

4 Click appropriate button (e.g., Find, Go Get It, Search, Seek, etc.) to begin search.

*The search service searches its index of Web pages for sites containing the text you entered. The search results appears in the **Explorer bar** on the left side of the screen.*

continued...

189

INTERNET TOOLS

Search the Web (cont.)

To select a different search provider:

- Click **Choose a Search Engine** list, then select the desired provider.

To go to a site listed in the search results:

- Click hyperlink to desired site in list that appears in the left pane.

Subscriptions

Internet Explorer supports subscriptions to Web content providers that deliver the content to your desktop on a regular basis. Subscriptions can be downloaded during off hours. Later, you can view the Web content offline (without making an Internet connection).

MANAGE SUBSCRIPTIONS

📖 *You can manage subscriptions from Internet Explorer or from any folder window.*

1 Click **Favorites** menu.. Alt + A

2 Click **Manage Subscriptions**... M

*The **Subscriptions** folder window appears.*

✓ *If you change the view of this folder's item to **Details** (see **Change View of Folder Icons**, page 92), you can view useful information about the subscription, such as the last update, status, next update, schedule, and priority.*

3 Right-click icon for desired subscription.

4 Select desired option:

- **Open** .... O

  to open subscription Web page.

INTERNET TOOLS

Manage Subscriptions (cont.)

- **Update Now** .... U

  to update subscription information now.

- **Copy** C

  to copy the subscription.

- **Delete** .... D

  to delete the subscription.

- **Properties** .... R

  to change subscription properties (receiving, and scheduling options).

UPDATE ALL SUBSCRIPTIONS

1 Click **Favorites** menu .... Alt + A

2 Click **Update All Subscriptions** .... U

Create Desktop Shortcut to a Web Page

Create a shortcut icon on the desktop that, when clicked, connects to the specified Web site.

📖 *If Internet Explorer isn't running when you click the shortcut, it automatically opens and connects to your Internet service provider.*

1 Open Internet Explorer to desired Web page.

2 Right-click desired Web page.

3 Click **Create Shortcut** .... T
   on shortcut menu that appears.

4 Click [OK] .... Enter

191

INTERNET TOOLS

Print Current Web Page

- Click 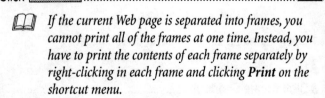 .... Ctrl + P
  on **Standard** toolbar.

  OR

  a Click **File** menu .... Alt + F

  b Click **Print** .... P

  OR

  a Right-click Web page to print.

  b Click **Print** I
  on shortcut menu that appears.

  OR

  a Right-click on hyperlink to Web page you
  want to print.

  b Click **Print Target** .... P
  on shortcut menu that appears.

  *The **Print** dialog box appears.*

2 Click ▒▒▒ OK ▒▒▒ .... Enter

> 📖 *If the current Web page is separated into frames, you
> cannot print all of the frames at one time. Instead, you
> have to print the contents of each frame separately by
> right-clicking in each frame and clicking **Print** on the
> shortcut menu.*

192

Save Current Web Page

1 Click **File** menu.. `Alt`+`F`

2 Click **Save As**.. `A`

Favorites Folder

The Favorites folder is available throughout Windows 98 so that you can add links not only to Web sites, but also to locations on your computer. You can access those links from within Internet Explorer, the Start menu, Windows Explorer, folder windows, and common dialog boxes.

ADD A FAVORITE

1 Open Web page or location on your computer
   that you want to add link to.

2 Click **Favorites** menu.. `Alt`+`A`

3 Click **Add to Favorites**... `A`

   The Add Favorite dialog box opens.

4 Select **No, just add the page**................................ `Alt`+`O`
   to my favorites option button.

5 Click `OK`... `Enter`

   The link is added to the Favorites menu.

OPEN A FAVORITE

⤶ From Internet Explorer

1 Click **Favorites** button on **Standard** toolbar .... `Favorites`

2 Click desired link in **Favorites bar** (left pane)
   to view Web page in right pane.

   OR

   a Click folder containing favorite to open.

   b Click desired favorite.

continued...

INTERNET TOOLS

Open a Favorite (cont.)

⌖ From the Start Menu

1 Click 🏁 Start .... 🏁

2 Point to **Favorites** .... 🔖 Favorites

3 Click favorite to open.

OR

a Click folder containing favorite to open.

b Click desired favorite.

⌖ From Any Folder Window

1 Click **Favorites** menu .... Alt + A

2 Click favorite to open.

OR

a Click folder containing favorite to open.

b Click desired favorite.

ADD NEW FOLDERS TO FAVORITES FOLDER

1 Start Internet Explorer. *See **Start Internet Explorer**, page 186.*

OR

Open any folder window.

2 Click **Favorites** menu .... Alt + A

3 Click **Organize Favorites** .... O

*The **Organize Favorites** dialog box appears.*

4 Click **Create New Folder** button ....

*A new folder icon appears in the **Organize Favorites** dialog box, with its name highlighted and the cursor blinking.*

5 Type folder name ....*name*

6 Press **Enter** .... Enter

7 Click Close .... Enter

DELETE A FAVORITE

1 Open any folder window.

2 Click **Favorites** menu.....................................`Alt` + `A`

3 Click **Organize Favorites**...............................`O`

The Organize Favorites dialog box appears.

4 Click favorite to delete.

5 Click `Delete`..`Alt` + `D`

OR

Press **Delete**..`Delete`

6 Click `Yes`..`Enter`

to send selected item to Recycle Bin.

MOVE A FAVORITE INTO ANOTHER FOLDER

1 Create new folder in which to store favorites,
  if necessary. *See **Add New Folders to Favorites
  Folder**, page 194.*

2 Drag favorite onto desired folder icon.

INTERNET TOOLS

OUTLOOK EXPRESS

Microsoft **Outlook Express** *is a component of Internet Explorer that integrates e-mail and newsgroup services for the exchange and organization of information. It supports multiple mail accounts and utilizes the* **Address Book** *to store and retrieve e-mail addresses.*

Launch Outlook Express

☞ From the Desktop

- Click **Outlook Express** icon..

☞ From Any Folder Window

1 Click **Go** menu.. `Alt` + `G`
2 Click **Mail** .... `M`

☞ From the Taskbar

- Click **Launch Outlook Express** button..
  on **Quick Launch** toolbar.

> *The first time you open Outlook Express, the* **Internet Connection Wizard** *will start if you have not yet set up an account with an Internet service provider (ISP).*

Run Internet Connection Wizard

Before you can use Outlook Express to send and receive e-mail, you must run the **Internet Connection Wizard** *to configure the program with your e-mail account information (user name, e-mail address, and mail server names). You may have already done this the first time you launched Outlook Express. If not, follow the steps below.*

1 Launch **Outlook Express**. *See* **Launch Outlook Express**, *above.*
2 Click **Tools** menu.. `Alt` + `T`
3 Point to **Accounts** .... `A`
4 Click **Mail** .... `M`

196

*The **Internet Accounts** dialog box appears.*

5 Click **Mail** tab .... Ctrl + Tab

6 Click Add ▶ .... Alt + A

7 Click **Mail** .... M

*The **Internet Connection Wizard** appears.*

8 Follow the wizard prompts carefully.

> 📖 *If you need help, contact your Internet Service
> Provider.*

Outlook Express Main Window

*When you first launch Outlook Express, the main window opens by
default. Below is a description of the main items contained in the
main window.*

> 📖 *If you prefer, you can have Outlook Express open
> directly to the **Mail** window, rather than the Main win-
> dow by selecting the **When starting, go directly to my
> Inbox folder** check box at the bottom of the main
> window. See **Read Messages**, page 202.*

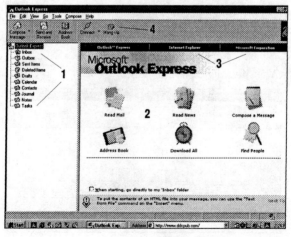

continued...

INTERNET TOOLS

Outlook Express Main Window (cont.)

❶ **Mail Folder list**	Appears in left column of the window when the Outlook Express main folder is selected.	
❷ **shortcuts**	Links to different e-mail functions, located in the center of the window.	
❸ **hyperlinks**	Links to Microsoft Home pages located at the top of the window.	
❹ **Outlook Express toolbar**	Displays buttons for common tasks.	

Compose and Send E-Mail Messages

✓ *To save online charges, you can compose your messages offline and send them later.*

1 Click **Compose Message** toolbar button......................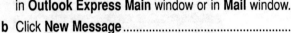

📖 *Click arrow to right of **Compose Message** button to select a stationery type.*

OR

a Click **Compose** menu...**Alt** + **C**
in **Outlook Express Main** window or in **Mail** window.

b Click **New Message**..**N**

The New Message window appears.

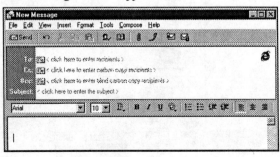

INTERNET TOOLS

Compose/Send E-Mail (cont.)

2 Type e-mail address(es) ....*address*
of message recipient(s) in **To** line.

> 📖 *You can click the icon next to the To line to select a*
> *recipient from the Address Book.*

3 Click either or both of the following boxes and enter the
recipient information as indicated:

- **Cc-> (Carbon Copy)** addresses of people who will
  receive copies of the message.

- **Bcc-> (Blind Carbon Copy)** same as Cc, except these
  names won't appear anywhere in the message, so other
  recipients won't know that the persons listed in the Bcc
  field received a copy.

4 Type message subject in **Subject** line...........................*subject*

5 Type your message in space provided..................................*text*

To send the message immediately:

- Click **Send** button.. 📧 Send

If you are not already online, Outlook Express automatically begins
connecting to your ISP. You may also be prompted for your e-mail
password.

To store the message in the Outbox for later delivery:

a Click **File** menu .... Alt + F

b Click **Send Later**.. L

The message is stored in your Outbox folder until you go online
and click the Send and Receive button on the Outlook Express
toolbar.

INTERNET TOOLS

Attach Files to E-Mail Messages

✐ From New Message Window

1 Click **attachments** icon ....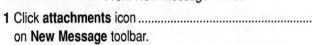
on **New Message** toolbar.

The Insert Attachment dialog box opens.

2 Select drive and folder(s) containing file to attach
from **Look in** list box.

3 Double-click folder in folders and files list to
open it, if necessary.

4 Select file to attach in the folders and files list.

5 Click Attach .... Alt + A

*The attachment will appear as an icon below the
body of the message.*

> ✓ *You can also drag a file, another e-mail message, or a
> hyperlink onto the New Message window to attach it.*

Retrieve New Messages

*Outlook Express connects to your ISP mail server and downloads
new e-mail messages to your computer.*

- Click **Send and Receive** toolbar button.......................... Send and Receive

*If you are not already connected to the Internet, Outlook Express
automatically begins connecting to your ISP, or a prompt will
display where you can click Yes to connect. You may also be
prompted to enter your e-mail password.*

*Once Outlook Express is connected to your ISP mail server, it
begins downloading new messages to your computer. A dialog box
displays the status of the transmittal. Retrieved messages are then
stored in the Inbox folder.*

View Messages in Mail Window

*You can read messages stored in your **Inbox**, **Outbox**, or any other mail folder from the **Mail** window.*

- Click icon for the folder whose contents you wish to view from **Mail Folders** list on left side of the **Outlook Express** screen.

*The **Mail** window opens with the contents of the selected folder displayed.*

The Mail Window

*When you click on a mail folder to display its contents, the **Mail** window opens. Below is a description of the items available in the Mail window.*

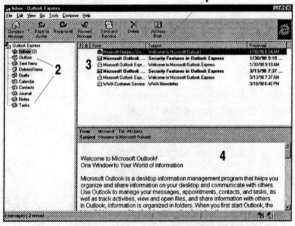

❶ The **Toolbar** provides access to frequently used commands.

❷ The **Folder list** shows the hierarchy of message folders. Plus signs (+) indicate expandable subfolders.

❸ The **Message list** shows a message after you select its folder.

❹ The **Preview pane and message header** shows information about and the content of a selected message in the **Message list** without opening it.

INTERNET TOOLS

Read Messages

1 Click on mail folder containing message you want to read to display its contents in **Message list** pane.

To read a message in the preview pane:

- Click once on desired message in **Message list**.

The message content appears in the lower half of the Mail window.

✓ *If the message content does not appear, select **Layout** on the **View** menu. In the dialog box that follows, select **Use preview pane** and click* OK

To open and read a message in a separate window:

- Double-click on desired message in **Message list**.

*The **Message** window opens, displaying the **Message** toolbar and the contents of the selected message.*

To close the Message window after reading a message:

- Click **Close** button..⊠
  in upper-right corner of window.

2 Use scroll bars in **Message** window or preview pane to view hidden parts of displayed message.

To read the next unread message:

a Click **View** menu ....Alt + V

b Point to **Next** ....N

c Click **Next Unread Message** ....M

OR

Click **Next** button on **Message** toolbar ....➡

if viewing message in **Message** window.

*Once you have read a message, it remains stored in the **Inbox** folder until you delete it or file it in another folder. See **Delete Messages** and **File a Message**, page 203.*

INTERNET TOOLS

Delete Messages

1 Select desired message from message
list in **Mail** window.

2 Click **Delete** button on **Mail** toolbar....................................

OR

1 Open desired message in **Message** window.

2 Click **Delete** button on **Message** toolbar...........................

File a Message

Move a to another message folder for future reference.

> ✓ *You can move a message quickly to a folder by drag-*
> *ging it from the Message list onto a folder icon in the*
> *folder list.*

1 Double-click desired message in **Message**
list to open it in its own message window.

2 Click **File** menu...

3 Click **Move to Folder** ....

The Move dialog box appears.

4 Click folder where you want to store message.

5 Click ....

INTERNET TOOLS

Create a New Message Folder

Create a message folder in which you can file related messages you want to keep.

          ☞ From Outlook Express

1 Click **File** menu.. `Alt`+`F`

2 Point to **Folder**.. `F`

3 Click **New Folder**... `N`

   *The **Create Folder** dialog box appears.*

4 Enter new folder name ....*name*

5 Select folder in which to create new folder.

6 Click ▮▮ OK ▮▮.. `Enter`

   The new folder appears in folder list; you can move folders into it.

Save a Message

1 Select desired message from **Message list** in **Mail** window.
   OR
   Open desired message in **Message** window.

2 Click **File** menu.. `Alt`+`F`

3 Click **Save As** .... `A`

   *The **Save Message As** dialog box appears.*

4 Select drive and folder(s) where you want to store
   the message file in **Save in** list box.

5 Click **File name** text box .... `Alt`+`N`

6 Type message name ....*name*

7 Click ▮ Save ▮ .... `Alt`+`S`

   *This procedure saves your message as a **Plain Text** file, which you can open in Notepad, Microsoft Word, or any word processing or text editor program. If you are saving an HTML-formatted message, you can save it in HTML format by clicking the drop-down arrow next to the **Save as type text** box and selecting **HTML Files**.*

204

Print a Message

✓ *You can bypass the **Print** dialog box and send the message to the printer using the most recently used print settings; open the message in the **Message** window and clicking the **Print** button 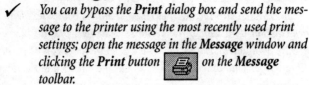 on the **Message** toolbar.*

1 Select message to print from **Message list** in **Mail** window.

OR

Double-click message to open it in **Message** window.

2 Click **File** menu .... `Alt` + `F`

3 Click **Print** .... `P`

*The **Print** dialog box appears.*

4 Select desired print options. *See **Customize Printer Settings**, page 229.*

5 Click ` OK ` .... `Enter`

NETWORKING

ABOUT NETWORKING

Windows 98 networking features let you connect computers with network cards or a modem. After you install the network hardware and software components, you will be able to share folders, files, printers, and messages with other users who are also connected to the network.

> *If an application or tool mentioned here is not installed on your system, see **Add or Remove Windows Components**, page 50, for information about installing it.*

Log On and Off a Network

*Access or close all network connections you may have established when you started Windows. If **User Profiles** is enabled, you can use the **Log Off** command to log on as a different user. If you have previously logged on as a user, the **Log Off** command will also indicate that user name.*

1 Click ![Start] .... 🏁

2 Click **L**og Off .... 🔑 Log Off

*The **Log Off Windows** dialog box appears.*

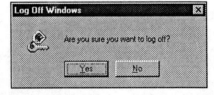

3 Click [Yes] when prompted... Y

4 Type **U**ser name and **P**assword as well as **D**omain name, if necessary, in **Enter Network Password** dialog box that appears.

5 Click [OK] .... Enter

Windows 98 closes all programs, validates your logon password, makes network connections, and then displays your desktop.

Set File and Print Sharing

Share your computer's files and printers with other computers on a network.

1 Open **Control Panel**. *See **Open Control Panel**, page 15.*

2 Click **Network** icon .... 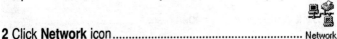 Network

*The **Network** dialog box appears.*

3 Click [File and Print Sharing] .... **Alt** + **F**

This button will be available only if you installed Microsoft's file and printer sharing service.

4 Select or deselect sharing options in dialog box that appears.

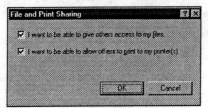

File and Print Sharing

☑ I want to be able to give others access to my files.

☑ I want to be able to allow others to print to my printer(s).

[OK] [Cancel]

5 Click [OK] .... Enter

Browse Network Computers

📖 *Unless folders or printers are shared, they will not appear when you are browsing network computers. See **Share a Folder or Drive**, page 211, and **Share a Printer**, page 222.*

⌖ From My Computer

1 Click **My Computer** icon on desktop .... My Computer

2 Click computer icon to open .... Chicago

continued...

NETWORKING

Browse Network Computers (cont.)

☞ From Network Neighborhood

1 Click **Network Neighborhood** icon .... Network Neighborhood
on desktop.

2 Click computer icon to open .... Chicago

✓ *If the computer you want to browse is not visible, click*
*the **Entire Network** icon, then click the **Network** icon*
the computer belongs to.

3 Click shared network folder .... 📁 or 📁
you want to open.

☞ From Any Folder Window

1 Click **Address bar** .... A
*See **Hide or Show Folder Toolbars**, page 132.*

2 Type or select path ....*computername**sharename*
to shared network folder in **Address bar** to open it.

☞ Using the Run Command

1 Open **Run** dialog box .... 🏁 + R

OR

a Click **Start** .... 🏁

b Click **Run** .... Run...

2 Type path ....*computer name**sharename*
to shared network folder.

OR

Type drive letter followed by a colon .... *drive:*
if network folder was mapped to a drive. *See **Map**
Network Drives, page 209.*

NETWORKING

Map Network Drives

Assign a drive letter to a shared network folder so you can access the network folder as you would a local network drive.

> 📖 *Instead of mapping a network drive, consider creating a shortcut to the shared folder. Then you can open the shared folder by clicking the shortcut. You can also use the **Map Drive** button on the folder toolbar. See **Create Shortcuts**, page 96.*

1 Click **Network Neighborhood** icon ....

> 📖 *If the **Network Neighborhood** folder window contains the computer icon you want to browse, go directly to step 4.*

2 Click **Entire Network** icon .... Entire Network
if necessary, to view computers in networks
to which you are connected.

3 Click network to open ....
if necessary.

If your computer is connected to multiple networks, each network is represented by an icon.

4 Click computer containing shared folder to map.

Drives on other computers appear as folder icons.

5 Right-click desired shared folder.

6 Click <u>M</u>ap Network Drive .... Ⓜ
on shortcut menu that appears.

continued...

NETWORKING

Map Network Drives (cont.)

*The **Map Network Drive** dialog box appears.*

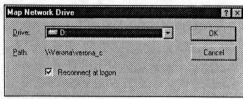

7 Select desired drive letter .... ⬆️ ⬇️
in **Drive** drop-down list.

> 📖 *If you select a drive letter that has already been
> mapped, the original mapping will be replaced.*

8 Select **Reconnect at logon** check box .... Alt + T
to reconnect each time you logon.

9 Click ▓ OK ▓ .... Enter

10 Close **Network Neighborhood** folder window.

*The mapped drive 🖥️ appears in the **My Computer** folder.*

ADD MAP DRIVE BUTTON TO FOLDER TOOLBAR

1 Click 🏁 Start .... 🔲

2 Point to **Settings** .... 🔧 Settings

3 Click **Folder Options** .... 📁 Folder Options...

*The **Folder Options** dialog box appears.*

4 Click **View** tab .... Ctrl + Tab

5 Select **Show Map Network Drive button
in toolbar** check box.

6 Click ▓ OK ▓

The following toolbar buttons appear in the folder window:

Map Drive   Disconnect

210

Share a Folder or Drive

*Windows 98 lets you share a folder or drive (and all its contents) with other users on a network. You can share folders from the desktop, any folder window, a common dialog box, the Find window result list, or Windows Explorer. To share folders with another computer, you must first enable **sharing** on your computer. See **Set File and Print Sharing**, page 207.*

1 Browse folders until folder or drive icon to share is in view.

2 Right-click folder or drive icon to share.

> *To share an entire drive, open the **My Computer** folder and right-click the drive you wish to share.*

3 Click **Sharing**..[H]

on shortcut menu that appears.

*The folder's **Properties** dialog box appears with **Sharing** tab selected.*

4 Select **Shared As** option button..............................[Alt]+[S]

5 Type or edit share name...*sharename*

in **Share Name** text box.

6 Type comment in **Comment** text box...........................*comment*

if desired.

> *The type of access rights (Share Level or User Level) available will depend upon your current access control setting. See **Set Network Sharing Access Control**, page 215.*

7 Set share-level access rights *(see page 212).*

OR

Set user-level access rights *(see page 212).*

8 Click [OK]...[Enter]

211

NETWORKING

SET SHARE-LEVEL ACCESS RIGHTS

Determine how users can use the files stored in the folder.

   ☞ From Sharing Tab in Folder's Properties Dialog Box

1 Select desired access type:

- **Read-Only** .... `Alt` + `R`

  enables other users to open and copy folders and files, but not to modify, move, or delete folders and files.

- **Full** .... `F`

  enables other users to add, modify, move, or delete folders and/or files.

- **Depends on Password** .... `D`

  allows different types of access for different users.

2 Type password(s), if desired.

> 📖 *If you specify password(s), Windows will prompt you to re-enter them to confirm when you close the dialog box.*

SET USER-LEVEL ACCESS RIGHTS

Specify which users can access files or printers you share. These users are listed on a master list maintained by a server, such as Windows NT.

> 📖 *User-level access rights require a connection to a network computer that maintains a list of users, such as a Windows NT server.*

   ☞ From Sharing Tab in Folder's Properties Dialog Box

To add a user or group:

1 Click `Add...` .... `Alt` + `A`

2 Select user name in **Name** list box.

212

3 Click appropriate access option button.

> 📖 *Access buttons include **Read Only**, **Full Access**, and **Custom**. If you select **Custom**, you will be prompted to specify access rights.*

4 Click [OK] .... Enter

To remove a user or group:

1 Select user name in **Name** list box.

2 Click [Remove...] .... Alt + R

To edit the rights for a user or group:

1 Select user name in **Name** list box.

2 Click [Edit...] .... Alt + E

NETWORK COMPONENTS AND SETTINGS

Add a Network Component

1 Click [Start] .... 🔲

2 Point to **Settings** .... Settings

3 Click **Control Panel** .... Control Panel

*The **Control Panel** window opens.*

4 Click **Network** icon .... Network

5 Click **Configuration** tab .... Ctrl + Tab

> 💣 *Improper changes to components on the **Configuration** tab can cause your network to work improperly. Therefore, consider recording the properties of each component before making changes.*

continued...

NETWORKING

Add Network Component (cont.)

6 Click [Add..] .... **Alt** + **A**

*The **Select Network Component Type** dialog box appears.*

7 Select desired component type.

8 Click [Add..] .... **Alt** + **A**

> 📖 *Subsequent options depend on the type of component you selected in step 7. Follow the prompts as instructed.*

9 Click [OK] .... **Enter**

Remove a Network Component

1 Click [Start] .... 🗐

2 Point to **Settings** .... Settings

3 Click **Control Panel** .... Control Panel

4 Click **Network** icon .... Network

*The **Network** dialog box appears.*

5 Click **Configuration** tab .... **Ctrl** + **Tab**

> 💣 *Improper changes to components on the **Configuration** tab can cause your network to work improperly. Therefore, consider recording the properties of each component before making changes.*

6 Select component to remove from list.

7 Click [Remove..] .... **Alt** + **R**

8 Click [OK] .... **Enter**

Enable Remote Administration of Your Computer

📖 *Remote administration requires user-level access control. See **Set Network Sharing Access Control**, below.*

1 Open **Passwords Properties** dialog box. *See **Open Password Properties Dialog Box**, page 216.*

2 Click **Remote Administration** tab .... `Ctrl` + `Tab`

3 Select **Enable remote** .... `Alt` + `E`
   administration of this server check box.

4 Click [Add...] .... `Alt` + `A`
   to select desired users or groups.

5 Click [OK] .... `Enter`

Set Network Sharing Access Control

Share-level access control gives you the option of assigning passwords to folders and printers you share on the network.

User-level access control requires a connection to a network computer that maintains a list of users, such as a Windows NT server. This system lets you efficiently manage permissions assigned to shared resources.

1 Open **Network** dialog box. *See **Open Network Dialog Box**, page 218.*

2 Click **Access Control** tab .... `Ctrl` + `Tab`

3 Select/deselect desired access control option buttons.

4 If you selected user-level access control, type name of computer or domain that maintain the master list of users.

5 Click [OK] .... `Enter`

NETWORKING

Change Primary Network Logon

Designate the network that will validate your logon to a network.

1 Open **Network** dialog box. *See **Open Network Dialog Box**, page 218.*

2 Click **Configuration** tab .... `Ctrl` + `Tab`

3 Select network to validate your password when you logon from **Primary Network Logon** list box.

4 Click [OK] .... `Enter`

Change Passwords and User Profiles

*The **Passwords** tool in **Control Panel** lets you change logon passwords, set user profiles, and enable remote administration of your computer.*

OPEN PASSWORDS PROPERTIES DIALOG BOX

1 Click [Start] .... 🎇

2 Point to **Settings** .... 🎇 Settings

3 Click **Control Panel** .... 📖 Control Panel

4 Click **Passwords** icon .... 🔑 Passwords

*The **Passwords Properties** dialog box appears.*

CHANGE WINDOWS PASSWORD

1 Open **Passwords Properties** dialog box *(see above)*.

2 Click **Change Passwords** tab .... `Ctrl` + `Tab`

3 Click [Change Windows Password] .... `W`

4 Select other password services to which you want to assign the same password.

📖 *When you assign the same password to other password services (such as Windows NT), you will receive only one logon prompt when logging on to Windows.*

5 Click ▐ OK ▐ .... Enter

6 Type passwords when prompted...............................*passwords*

7 Click ▐ OK ▐ .... Enter

A dialog box appears telling you that the passwords have been successfully changed.

📖 *Use the **Change Other Passwords** button to change the password for logon services independent of Windows, such as NetWare and Windows NT servers. Ask your network administrator for your password.*

SET UP USER PROFILES ON YOUR COMPUTER

1 Open **Passwords Properties** dialog box.
   *See **Open Passwords Properties Dialog Box**, page 216.*

2 Click **User Profiles** tab .... Ctrl + Tab

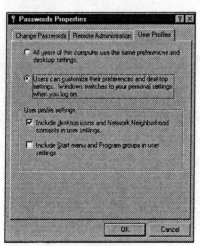

continued...

NETWORKING

Setup User Profiles (cont.)

3 Set desired check box for **User profile settings**.

4 Click [OK] .... Enter

Net Watcher 🖋 Net Watcher

Net Watcher is a Windows utility that lets you monitor, manage, and create network shares on your computer and administer network shares on a remote computer.

1 Click 🏁 Start .... 🏛

2 Point to **Programs** .... 📁 Programs

3 Point to **Accessories** .... 📁 Accessories

4 Point to **System Tools** .... 📁 System Tools

5 Click **Net Watcher** .... 🖋 Net Watcher

*The **Net Watcher** window opens.*

📖 *Consult the online Help feature for more instructions on working with Net Watcher.*

Change Network Settings

*From the **Network** dialog box, you can add, remove, and change the properties of network components.*

OPEN NETWORK DIALOG BOX

1 Click 🏁 Start .... 🏛

2 Point to **Settings** .... ⚙ Settings

3 Click **Control Panel** .... 🖥 Control Panel

4 Click **Network** icon .... 🖧 Network

*The **Network** dialog box appears.*

CHANGE OR VIEW NETWORK IDENTIFICATION INFORMATION

*The **computer name** should be unique, as it identifies your system on the network. The name cannot contain spaces. The **workgroup name** identifies the group of computers you will connect to. Check with your network administrator for the appropriate name.*

1 Open **Network** dialog box. *See **Open Network Dialog Box**, page 218.*

2 Click **Identification** tab .... `Ctrl` + `Tab`

3 Type or view information in text boxes provided.

4 Click OK .... `Enter`

CHANGE OR VIEW NETWORK COMPONENT PROPERTIES

1 Open **Network** dialog box. *See **Open Network Dialog Box**, page 218.*

2 Click **Configuration** tab .... `Ctrl` + `Tab`

> 💣 *Improper changes to components on the **Configuration** tab can cause your network to work improperly. Therefore, consider recording the properties of each component before making changes.*

3 Select desired component type.

4 Click **Properties** .... `Alt` + `R`

Options depend on the component you select. The following table lists frequently used components and settings.

Icon	Component Name
Clients	(Microsoft Network) provide the software that enables your computer to connect to other computers.

continued...

NETWORKING

Network Component Properties (cont.)

Adapters

(Ethernet, Dial-Up, TV Data)
physically connect your computer to a network,
such as a network card or modem.

Protocols

(NetBEUI, TCP/IP, IPX/SPX)
provide the languages that the devices use to
communicate with each other. For example, TCP/IP
is the language of the Internet. Therefore, you
typically "bind" the Dial-Up Adapter to communicate
with this protocol.

Services

(File and printer sharing for Microsoft Networks)
provide the software that enables your computer to
share files and printers.

*Typically, the network components are installed automatically
when you install Windows, or when you install a network card.*

5 Click ....

NETWORK PRINTERS

Windows 98 lets you share printers with other users on a network.

Add Network Printer

Install a printer that you can access through a network.

> *You can also install a network printer from the*
> ***Printers** folder. See **Add Local Printer**, page 224. The*
> *advantage of using the above procedure is that you do*
> *not have to supply the manufacturer, name of the*
> *printer, or the network path to the printer.*

1 Browse **Network Neighborhood** ....
to locate and open the computer sharing
printer you want to install.

2 Right-click shared printer.

3 Click <u>I</u>nstall ....
on shortcut menu that appears.

*The **Add Printer Wizard** dialog box appears.*

4 Click `Yes` or `No` .... **Y**/**N**

> 📖 *If you click* `Yes` *(indicating that you print from MS-DOS based programs), an additional dialog box appears. Click* `Capture Printer Port...` *then select the port to which you want to assign the network printer in the **Device** list box, and click* `OK` *When you capture a printer port, you can print to a network printer from an MS-DOS application by selecting the port assigned in this Printer Wizard step.*

5 Click `Next >` to continue..................................... **Enter**

6 Click command buttons as desired to navigate through wizard:

- `Next >` .... **Enter**

- `< Back` .... **B**

- `Cancel` .... **Esc**

7 If prompted, select **Keep existing driver** option button .... **K**

8 Type printer name in **Printer name** box.

9 Click `Yes` if you want this printer used by default.

10 Click `Next >` .... **Enter**

11 Click `Yes` if you want to print a test page.

12 Click `Finish` .... **Enter**

*Windows adds a printer icon in the **Printers** folder, and the printer will be available from all Windows applications.*

Networking

Share a Printer

Windows 98 lets you share a printer with others on a network. Once shared, other users can send documents to your printer as if it were their own. To share printers, you must first enable sharing on your computer. See Set File and Print Sharing, page 207.

1 Click **Start** .... 🏁

2 Point to **Settings** .... 🔧 S̲ettings

3 Click **Printers** .... 🖨 P̲rinters

4 Right-click icon of printer to share.

5 Click **Sharing** .... H
on shortcut menu that appears.

*The printer's **Properties** dialog box appears.*

6 Select **Shared As** option button .... Alt + S

7 Type or edit proposed share name ....*sharename*
in **Share Name** text box.

8 Type comment in **Comment** text box, if desired.

📖 *The type of access rights (Share Level or User Level) available will depend upon your current access control setting. See **Set Network Sharing Access Control**, page 215.*

9 Set share-level access rights *(see page 223)*.

OR

Set user-level access rights *(see page 223)*.

10 Click ▓ OK ▓ .... Enter

SET SHARE-LEVEL ACCESS RIGHTS

Determine how users can use the shared printer.

1 Type password(s), if desired, in **Password** text box.

2 Click [OK] .... Enter

> 📖 *You will be prompted to retype the password when you click [OK] or [Apply]. If you specify a password, other users will have to supply the password to use your printer.*

SET USER-LEVEL ACCESS RIGHTS

Specify which users can have access to each file or printer you share. These users are listed on a master list and do not need a password to use shared files and printers.

> 📖 *User-level access rights require a connection to a net-work computer that maintains a list of users, such as a Windows NT server.*

  ↳ From Sharing Tab in Printer's Properties Dialog Box

To add a user or group:

1 Click [Add] .... Alt + A

2 Select user name in **Name** list box.

3 Select **Full Access** command button .... F

4 Click [OK]

To remove a user or group:

1 Select user name in **Name** list box.

2 Click [Remove] .... Alt + R

223

Printers and Fonts

MANAGE PRINTERS

Windows 98 lets you add and remove printers from your computer, rename them, set the default printer, select operating options, and set printers to work offline.

Open Printers Folder

You can accomplish all printer management tasks, such as deleting, renaming, and setting a printer as the default printer, from the Printers folder.

1 Click **Start** .... 🏁

2 Point to **Settings** .... 🖳 Settings

3 Click **Printers** .... 🖨 Printers

📖 *You can also access the Printers folder from the My Computer folder. See My Computer, page 22.*

Add Local Printer

When you add a printer, Windows 98 adds an an icon in the Printers folder for the printer that is physically connected to your computer. Windows will then recognize the printer, allowing you to print documents to that printer, as well as manage its settings and activities.

📖 *Before starting, make certain your printer is connected properly. See your printer documentation for help with this.*

1 Open **Printers** folder *(see above)*.

2 Click **Add Printer** icon .... 📇 Add Printer

The Add Printer Wizard dialog box appears.

3 Click **Next >** .... Enter

📖 *You can click Next, or Back, or Cancel at any time.*

4 Select **Local printer** option button.

PRINTERS AND FONTS

Add Local Printer (cont.)

5 Click [Next >] .... [Enter]

6 Select your printer's manufacturer from **Manufacturers** list box.

7 Select your printer model in **Printers** list.

📖 *If you have floppy disks for your printer software, click* [Have Disk] *and follow the prompts.*

8 Click [Next >] .... [Enter]

9 Select port where your computer is connected in list (typically LPT1).

10 Click [Next >] .... [Enter]

11 Type or edit printer name ....*name* in **Printer name** text box if desired.

12 Click **Yes** option button if you want this printer used by default.

13 Click [Next >] .... [Enter]

14 Select **Yes** option button if you want to print a test page.

15 Click [Finish] .... [Enter]

*Windows 98 will add a printer icon in the **Printers** folder, and the printer will be available in all Windows applications when you choose to print.*

✓ *You can add multiple printer icons for the same physical printer and then apply different settings to each.*

PRINTERS AND FONTS

Delete Local Printer

*You can remove a printer's icon from the **Printers** folder. Once it is deleted, however, you cannot print to that printer or manage its settings and activities.*

1 Open **Printers** folder. *See **Open Printers Folder**, page 224.*

2 Right-click desired printer icon.

   OR

   a Select desired printer icon ....

   b Click **File** menu .... Alt + F

3 Click **Delete** .... D

4 Click Yes .... Enter

   to confirm your deletion.

Rename Printer

1 Open **Printers** folder. *See **Open Printers Folder**, page 224.*

2 Right-click desired printer icon.

   OR

   a Select desired printer icon ....

   b Click **File** menu .... Alt + F

3 Click **Rename** .... M

   Windows 98 highlights the current name and a cursor appears at the end of the name.

4 Type or edit printer name as desired ....*name*

5 Click any blank area on the workspace when finished.

   OR

   Press **Enter** .... Enter

PRINTERS AND FONTS

Set Printer to Work Offline

This option is available for network printers or printers added to a portable computer. When you print to an offline printer, Windows stores the documents in a local printer queue until your computer has access to the printer.

1 Open **Printers** folder. *See **Open Printers Folder**, page 224.*

2 Right-click icon of printer ....
you want to work offline.

OR

  a Select desired printer icon ....

  b Click **File** menu... `Alt` + `F`

3 Select **Work Offline** .... `O`

A check mark indicates the printer is set to work offline.

Windows 98 will notify you when the printer is available. You can then complete the print jobs that are stored in the Printer Queue.

Pause or Restart a Printer

☞ From the Printers Folder

1 Open **Printers** folder. *See **Open Printers Folder**, page 224.*

2 Select icon of printer ....
you want to pause or restart.

3 Click **File** menu... `Alt` + `F`

4 Select **Pause Printing**.. `A`
to pause printer.

A check mark next to this option indicates the printer is paused.

OR

Deselect **Pause Printing**.. `A`
to restart printer.

227

Printers and Fonts

Select Printer Options

1 Open **Printers** folder. *See Open Printers Folder, page 224.*

2 Right-click desired printer in **Printers** folder.

3 Click desired option(s) on shortcut menu that appears:

- **Open** .... [O]

  opens the printer queue.

- **Pause Printing** (local printer only) .... [A]

  pauses the print document.

- **Set as Default** .... [F]

  specifies that the selected printer will be used
  automatically if no other printer is selected.

- **Purge Print Document** .... [G]

  deletes the print documents from the printer queue.

- **Use Printer Offline** (network printer only) .... [U]

  sets network or laptop printer for use when it is not
  currently connected or available on your system. When
  you send documents to an offline printer, they are stored
  until you activate the printer by selecting the Use Printer
  Offline command that appears the next time you
  open the shortcut menu. See Set Printer to Work Offline,
  page 227.

- **Sharing** (local printer only) .... [H]

  displays the sharing properties for the printer.

- **Create Shortcut** .... [S]

  creates a printer shortcut to a printer on the desktop.

- **Delete** .... [D]

  deletes printer. If you delete a printer, you can
  always add it again. See Add Local Printer, page 224,
  and Add Network Printer, page 220.

PRINTERS AND FONTS

Select Printer Options (cont.)

- **Rename** .... M

  *renames printer. After you select this command,
  you can edit the name that appears below the icon.
  See* **Rename Printer**, *page 226.*

- **Properties** .... R

  lets you set printer options. See **Customize Printer
  Settings**, *below.*

  > *You can also access printer management commands
  > by selecting them from the* **File** *menu in the*
  > **Printers** *folder.*

Customize Printer Settings

From the printer **Properties** *dialog box, you can set numerous printer
options. For example, depending on your printer, you may set options
for the following categories: General, Details, Color Management,
Sharing, Paper, Graphics, or Device Options. Options depend on the
printer selected.*

SET PRINTER PROPERTIES

1 Click **Start** .... 📖

2 Point to **Settings** .... Settings

3 Click **Printers** .... Printers

  The **Printers** *folder window opens.*

  > *You can also access the* **Printers** *folder from the* **My
  > Computer** *folder. See* **My Computer**, *page 22.*

4 Right-click desired printer icon.

5 Click **Properties** .... R
  on shortcut menu that appears.

  The printer **Properties** *dialog box appears.*

continued...

PRINTERS AND FONTS

Printer Properties (cont.)

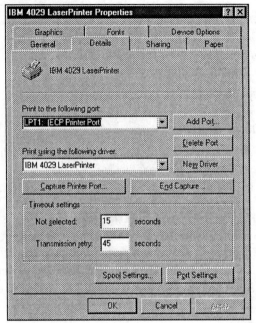

6 Select desired dialog box tab ....
from the following:

- **Details** to select printer port and driver options.
- **Device Options** to select options, such as printer memory, that are unique to the selected printer.
- **Fonts** to select font settings and/or cartridge options.
- **General** to select printer name, comment, and separator page options.
- **Graphics** to select settings for printing graphics.
- **Paper** to select paper size, location, and orientation options.
- **PostScript** to select settings for postscript printers.
- **Sharing** to select printer sharing options.

PRINTERS AND FONTS

7 Set options on selected tab(s) as desired.

 See the tables below for descriptions of some of the options that might be available on the General, Details and Paper tabs. The properties found on other tabs are not covered.

8 Click when finished .... Enter

Description of Common Printer Properties

GENERAL PRINTER PROPERTIES

With this setting:	You can:
Comment	Type a comment to appear with the printer when other users connect to it, such as a description of the printer location and the time it is available.
Separator page	Insert a page that identifies the owner of print files. Choose between a full page that includes graphics or a simple page with text only.
Browse	Locate and specify which file you want to use as a separator page.
	You can set up separator pages only if a printer is attached directly to your computer.
Print Test Page	Test the printer.

PRINTERS AND FONTS

PRINTER DETAILS

A *printer port* is an access point between the application software and the printer. A *printer driver* is the software that enables the application software to access the printer port. It converts an application's printer request into a language the printer understands.

With this setting:	You can:
Print to the following port	Change printer port by selecting the desired port from the list or by typing the network path.
Add Port	Add a port or specify a network path.
Delete Port	Delete a printer port.
Print using the following driver	Display the type of printer you are using.
New Driver	Change or update the printer driver.
Capture Printer Port	Map a local port (assign a path) to a shared network printer.
End Capture	Remove the mapping of a local port to a shared network printer.
Timeout settings	
Not selected	Type the number of seconds Windows 98 will wait before reporting that the printer is offline.
Transmission retry	Type the number of seconds Windows 98 will wait before reporting that the printer is not ready for the next part of the file.
Spool Settings	Select how the file is sent to the printer.
Port Settings	View or change the printer port settings.

PRINTERS AND FONTS

PRINTER PAPER PROPERTIES

With this setting:	You can:
Paper si_z_e	Select a paper or envelope size from the list.
Orientation	
A _P_ortrait	Select to print in tall paper orientation.
A _L_andscape	Select to print in wide paper orientation.
Paper _s_ource	Select where the printer's paper is located.
_C_opies	Type or select the number of copies for each print job.
Unp_r_intable Area	Set margins.
A_b_out	View your printer software's copyright information.
Restore _D_efaults	Restore the original paper settings.

*To read about a setting, click the **Help** button* 🔳 *in the upper right corner of the **Properties** dialog box, then click the setting you want help with. When you click the **Help** button, the pointer becomes a* ⬚?

PRINTERS AND FONTS

Manage Printer Queues

Windows 98 provides commands for managing print documents (files sent to a printer). For example, you can cancel or change the order of print documents in a printer queue.

OPEN PRINTER QUEUE WINDOW

*The **Printer Queue** window displays all the print jobs currently being processed by your computer.*

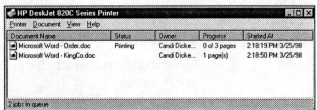

1 Open **Printers** folder. *See **Open Printers Folder**, page 224.*

2 Click desired printer icon ....

> 📖 *Print documents appear in the **Printer Queue** window in the order they were sent.*

Cancel or Pause Print Documents

1 Open **Printers** folder. *See **Open Printers Folder**, page 224.*

2 Click the desired printer icon ....
to open its print queue.

3 Right-click print document to cancel or pause in the list.

4 Click desired option from shortcut menu that appears:

- **P**ause Printing .... `A`
- **C**ancel Printing... `C`

> 📖 *You can pause or cancel any print document sent to a printer physically connected to your computer. For network printers, you can only pause or cancel **your own** documents in this way.*

PRINTERS AND FONTS

Purge Print Documents

When you purge print documents, you cancel all print jobs currently being processed on the selected printer.

1 Open the **Printers** folder. *See **Open Printers Folder**, page 224.*

2 Click the desired printer icon .... to open its print queue.

3 Click **Printer** menu ....`Alt`+`P`

4 Click **Purge Print Documents** ....`G`

> 📖 *You can only purge print documents that are **waiting** to be printed. You can only purge **your own** documents from a printer queue on a network printer.*

Change Print Documents Order

1 Open the **Printers** folder. *See **Open Printers Folder**, page 224.*

2 Click the desired printer icon .... to open its print queue.

3 Drag and drop desired print document into preferred location in list.

> 📖 *You can only change the order of print documents that are **waiting** to be printed. You cannot change the order of print documents on a network printer.*

PRINTERS AND FONTS

WORK WITH FONTS

Windows 98 lets you preview the fonts that are installed on your computer. You may also add and remove fonts on your computer.

Add and Remove Fonts

*Windows 98 stores fonts in the **Fonts** folder, a system folder that displays and manages the fonts installed on your system. The fonts listed in the **Fonts** folder will be available in all Windows applications.*

OPEN FONTS FOLDER

1 Click [🏁 Start] .... 📣

2 Point to **Settings** .... 🗀 Settings

3 Click **Control Panel** .... 🖳 Control Panel

4 Click **Fonts** folder icon .... 🎵 Fonts

5 Click **View** menu .... [Alt] + [V]
  to organize and view fonts as you prefer:

  ▪ **Large Icons** .... [G]

  shows fonts as large icons.

  ▪ **List** .... [L]

  shows fonts as small icons.

  ▪ **List Fonts By Similarity** .... [S], [S], [Enter]

  groups similar fonts together.

  ▪ **Details** .... [D]

  lists font file name, size, and modification date and lets you quickly sort fonts by clicking the column headings.

  OR

  Select the desired toolbar view button:

shows fonts as large icons.

 shows fonts as small icons.

 groups similar fonts together.

 lists font file name, size, and modification date and lets you quickly sort fonts by clicking the column headings.

PREVIEW FONTS

1 Open **Fonts** folder. *See* ***Open Fonts Folder***, *page 236.*

2 Double-click desired font file .... 🆃 or Ⓐ

*The **Font Preview** window appears.*

To print sample of a font:

- Click Print .... Ⓟ
  in **Font Preview** window.

To close the Font preview window:

- Click Done .... Ⓓ
  in **Font Preview** window.

Printers and Fonts

INSTALL NEW FONTS

You can install new fonts to your hard drive so they are available in all applications.

1 Open the **Fonts** folder. *See **Open Fonts Folder**, page 236.*

2 Click **File** menu..`Alt`+`F`

3 Click **Install New Font** ....`I`

*The **Add Fonts** dialog box appears.*

4 Select drive where font files are stored from **Drives** list box.

5 Select folder where font files are stored from **Folders** list box.

6 Select fonts you want to install.

> ✓ *Press* `Ctrl` *while clicking fonts to select multiple fonts at one time (see **Select Folders and Files**, page 166), or click* `Select All` *to select all font files in the current folder.*

7 Click `OK` ....`Enter`

PRINTERS AND FONTS

REMOVE FONTS

When you delete fonts from you hard disk, they are permanently deleted.

1 Open the **Fonts** folder. *See* ***Open Fonts Folder****, page 236.*

2 Select fonts to delete.

✓ *Press* Ctrl *while clicking fonts to select multiple fonts at one time. See* ***Select Folders and Files****, page 166.*

3 Right-click selected font(s).

4 Click **Delete** .... D

5 Click Yes at prompt .... Y

Fonts are also listed in the ***Windows*** *folder in the left pane of Windows Explorer.*

INDEX

INDEX

I

INDEX

V

W